05.14.03— SITTING ALONE IN THE VW, WAITING FOR MY SISTER TO RETURN FROM AN ERRAND AT A FRIEND'S HOUSE, I STARTED DRAWING THE STREET SIGN JUST AHEAD OF THE CAR. BY THE END OF THE DAY, I FINISHED THE PAGE WITH A SMALL DRAWING OF A CERAMIC GOLDFISH WHICH HUNG ON MY BEDROOM WALL. OVER THE NEXT FEW MONTHS, I TOOK MY SKETCHBOOK EVERYWHERE AND FOUND IT PARTICULARLY ENGAGING WHEN I WAS ALONE IN RESTAURANTS AND COFFEE SHOPS.

GRADUALLY, THE PAGES TOOK ON A LIFE OF THEIR OWN. THEY REFLECTED MY THOUGHTS AND MOODS. THEY RECORDED RANDOM EVENTS. THEY INCIDENTALLY BECAME A COLLAGE OF PERSONAL HISTORY AND MEMORY.

THIS IS A COMPILATION OF MY FAVORITE PAGES. THEY SPAN THREE YEARS, TWO SKETCHBOOKS, ONE HUNDRED AND SIXTY PAGES, FOUR LIVING SITUATIONS, TWO CARS, THREE COLLEGES, TWENTY-TWO STATES, SEVEN HAIRSTYLES, COUNTLESS PENS, AND ONE LIFE-CHANGING LOVE EMBODIED IN A SKELETON KEY. THEY ARE THE TRUTH AS I HAVE KNOWN IT.

Amelia Harnas   05.30.06

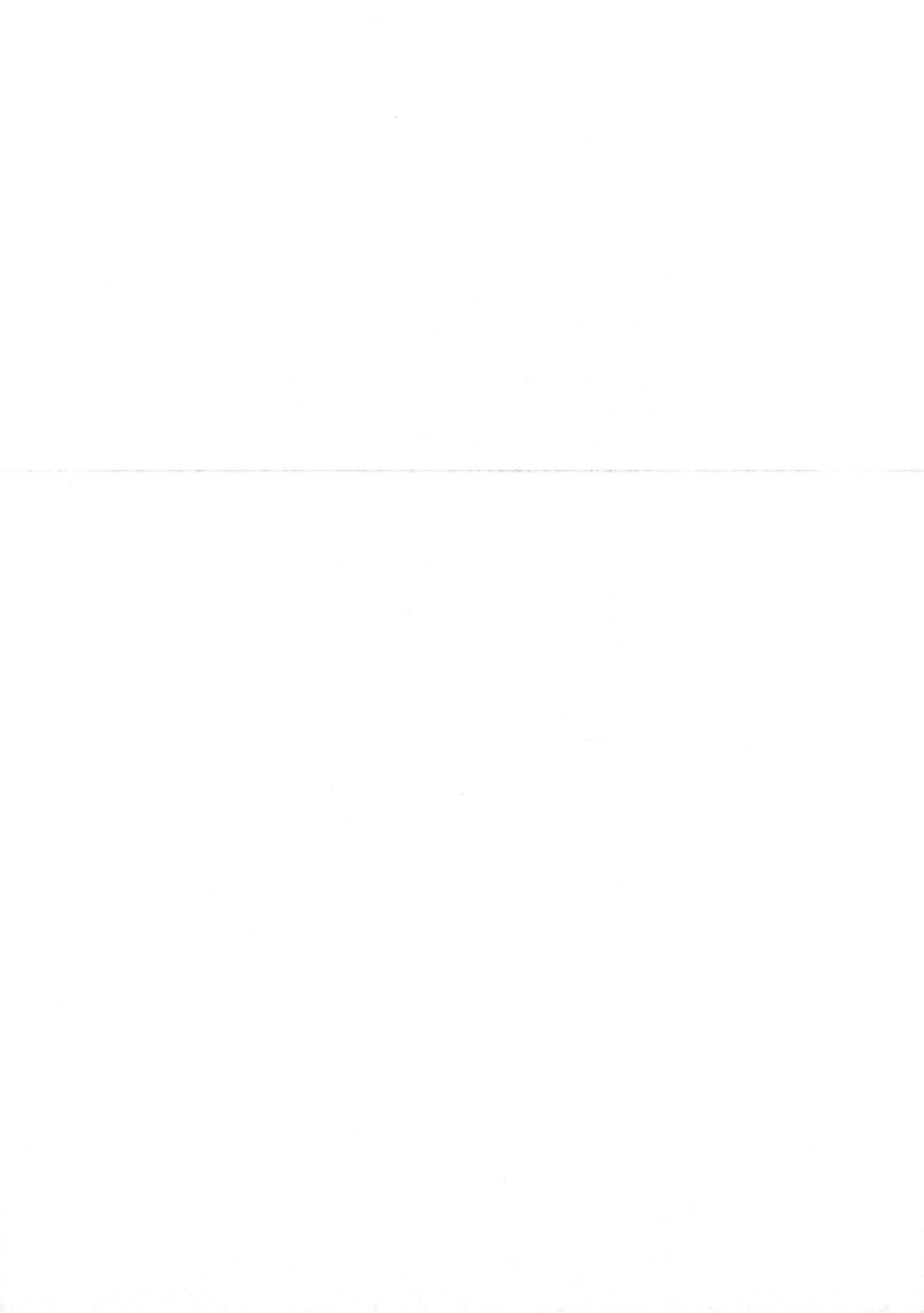

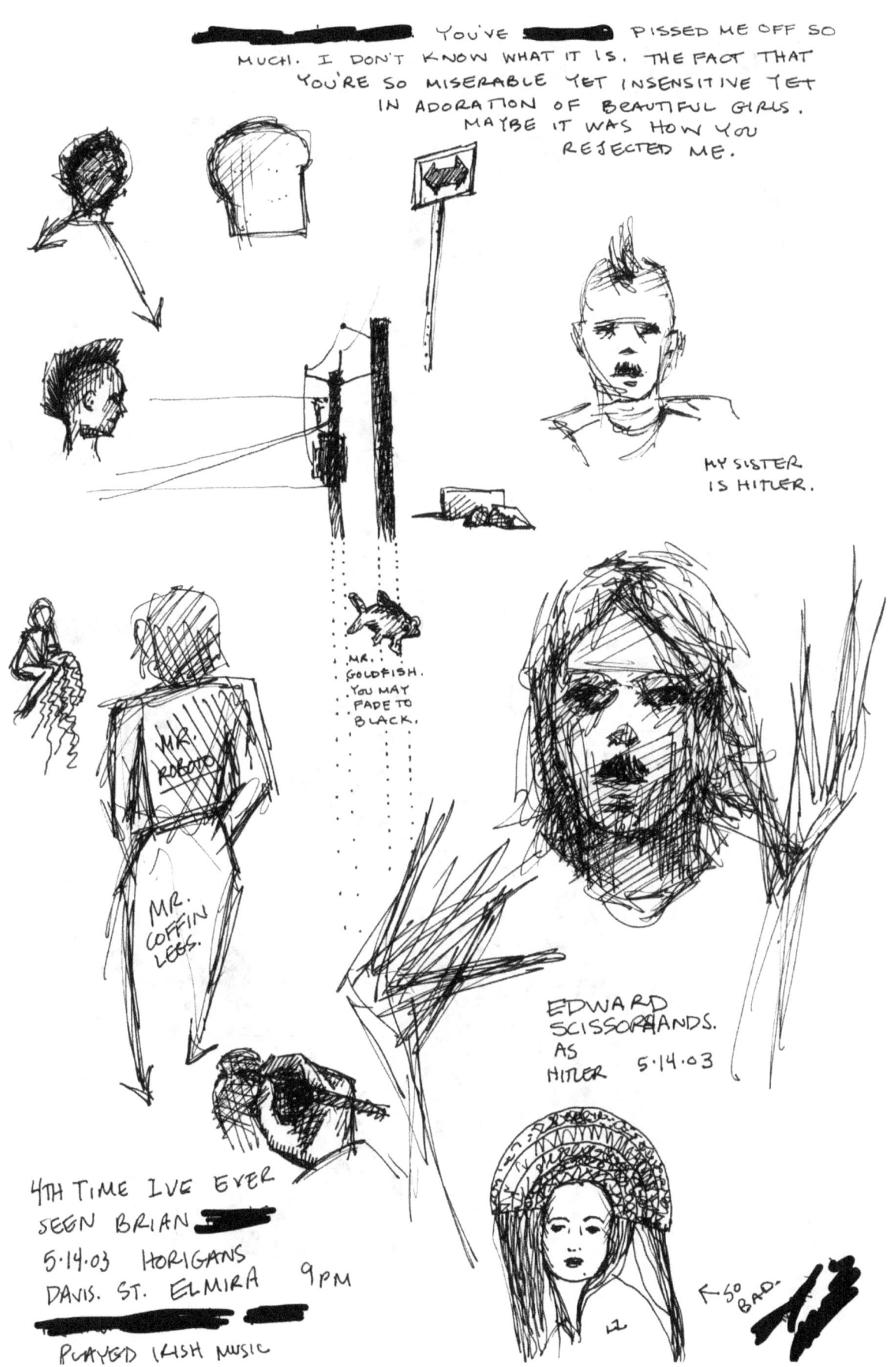

YOU'VE ███ PISSED ME OFF SO MUCH. I DON'T KNOW WHAT IT IS. THE FACT THAT YOU'RE SO MISERABLE YET INSENSITIVE YET IN ADORATION OF BEAUTIFUL GIRLS. MAYBE IT WAS HOW YOU REJECTED ME.

MY SISTER IS HITLER.

MR. GOLDFISH. YOU MAY FADE TO BLACK.

MR. ROBOTO

MR. COFFIN LEGS.

EDWARD SCISSORHANDS. AS HITLER 5·14·03

4TH TIME I'VE EVER SEEN BRIAN ███
5·14·03 HORIGANS
DAVIS. ST. ELMIRA 9PM
PLAYED IRISH MUSIC

← SO BAD.

creepy

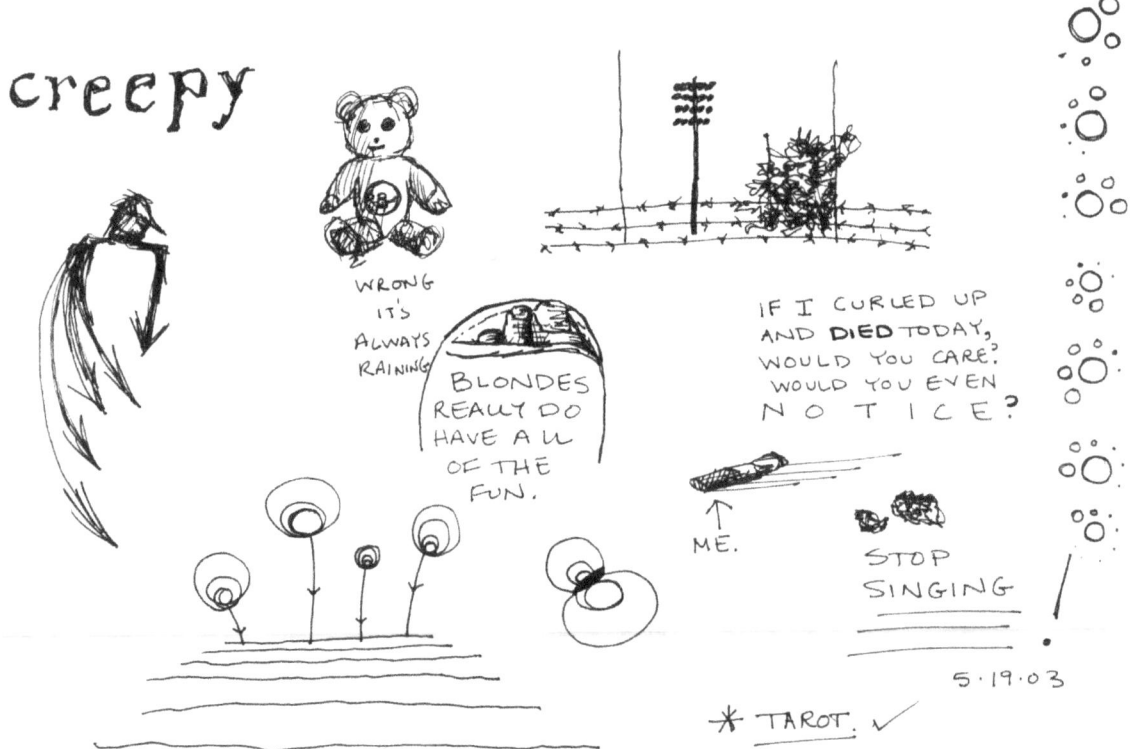

WRONG
IT'S
ALWAYS
RAINING

BLONDES
REALLY DO
HAVE ALL
OF THE
FUN.

IF I CURLED UP
AND **DIED** TODAY,
WOULD YOU CARE?
WOULD YOU EVEN
N O T I C E ?

↑
ME.

STOP
SINGING

5·19·03

* TAROT. ✓

Color is its own reward.
— CROWDED HOUSE

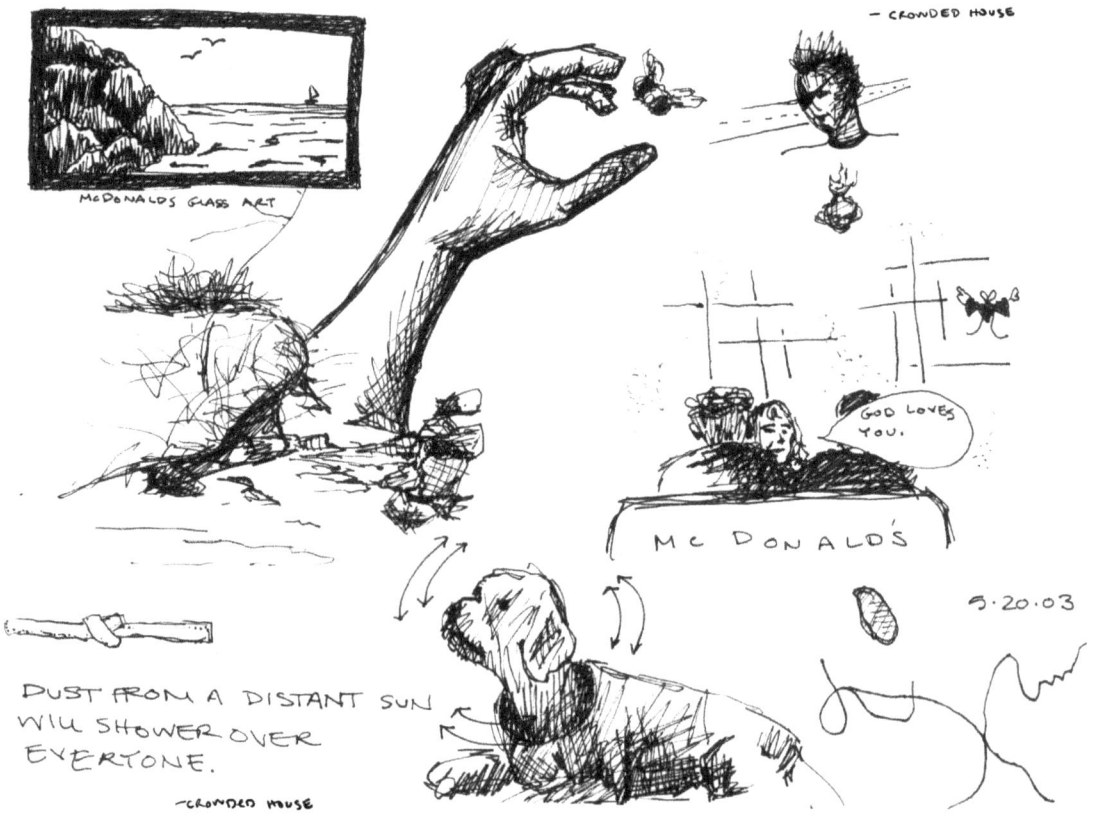

McDONALDS GLASS ART

GOD LOVES
YOU.

McDONALD'S

5·20·03

DUST FROM A DISTANT SUN
WILL SHOWER OVER
EVERYONE.

—CROWDED HOUSE

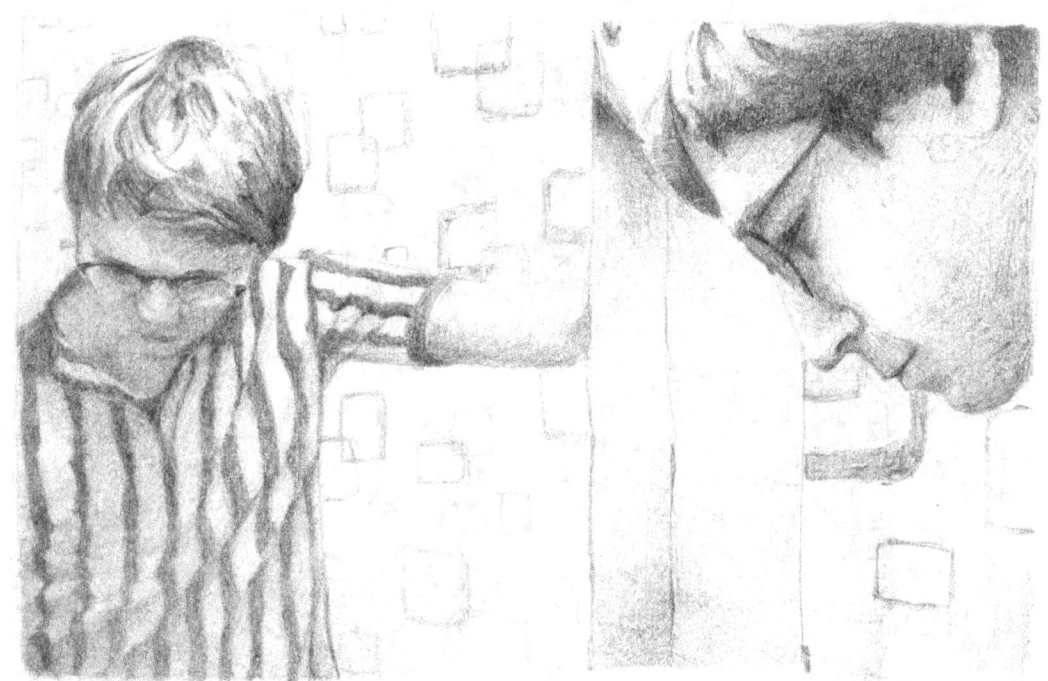

I AM SO OUT OF IT.
5·24·03

PHOTO BY:
CATHERINE TOEWS

Ever find stars
DARK & INVISIBLE
beneath bridges.
HIDDEN
they're a differ-
IN
ent type of star.
THE
You can only he-
DRAINSPOUTS
ar them - never
ECHOING
see them shine.

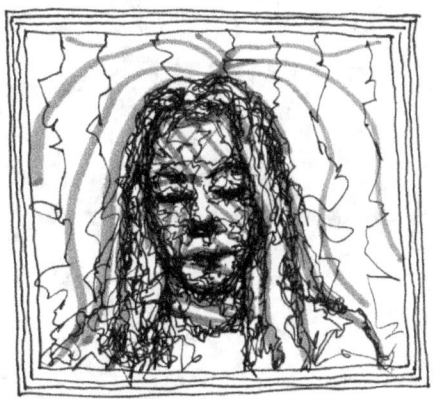

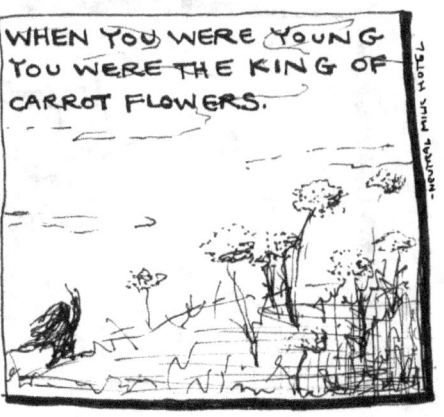

WHEN YOU WERE YOUNG
YOU WERE THE KING OF
CARROT FLOWERS.

— NEUTRAL MILK HOTEL

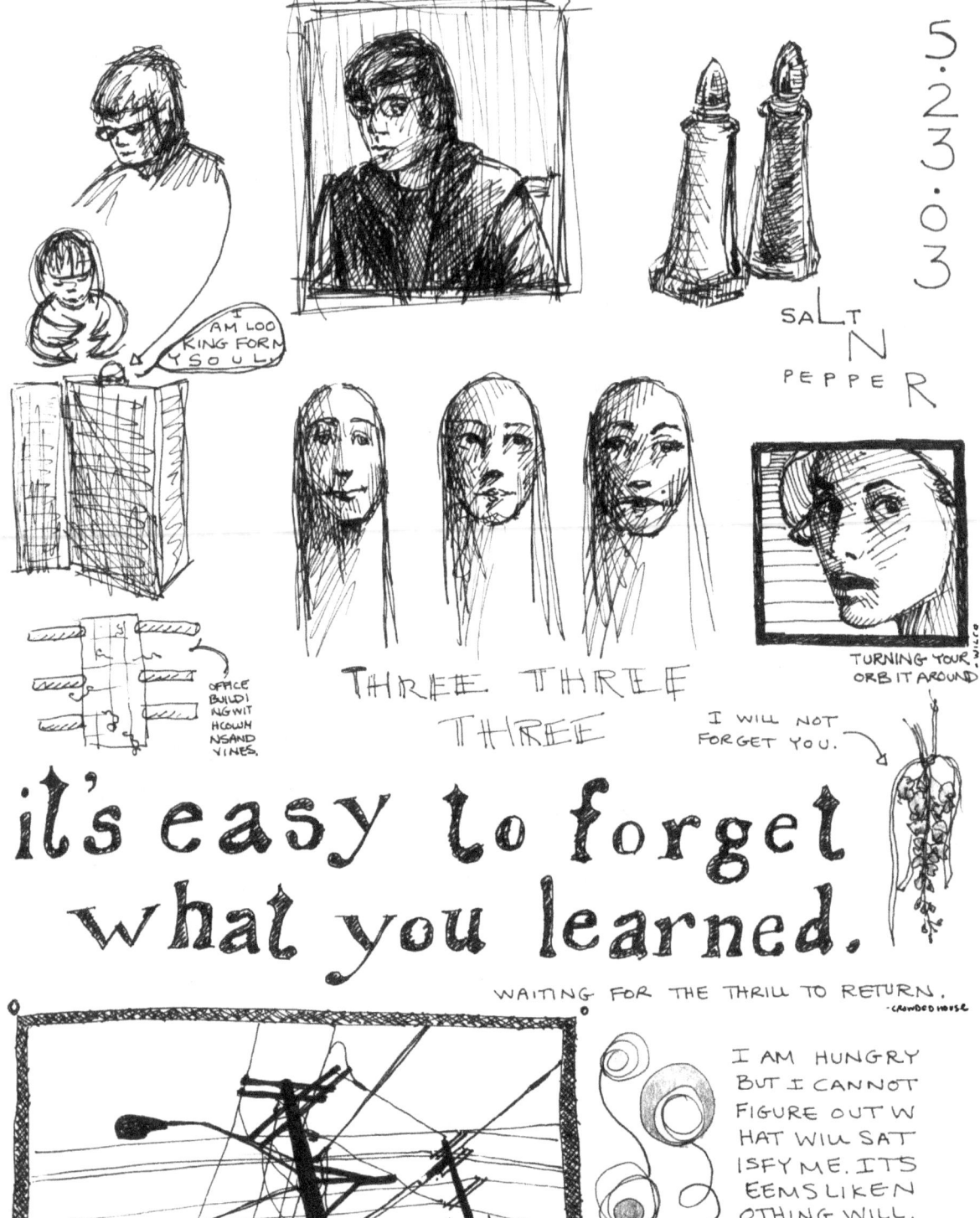

5.30.03

SALT N PEPPER

I AM LOOKING FORM Y SOUL

OFFICE BUILDING WITH COWN NSAND VINES.

THREE THREE THREE

TURNING YOUR ORBIT AROUND. WILCO

I WILL NOT FORGET YOU.

it's easy to forget what you learned.

WAITING FOR THE THRILL TO RETURN.
- CROWDED HOUSE

I AM HUNGRY BUT I CANNOT FIGURE OUT WHAT WILL SATISFY ME. ITS EEMS LIKEN OTHING WILL.

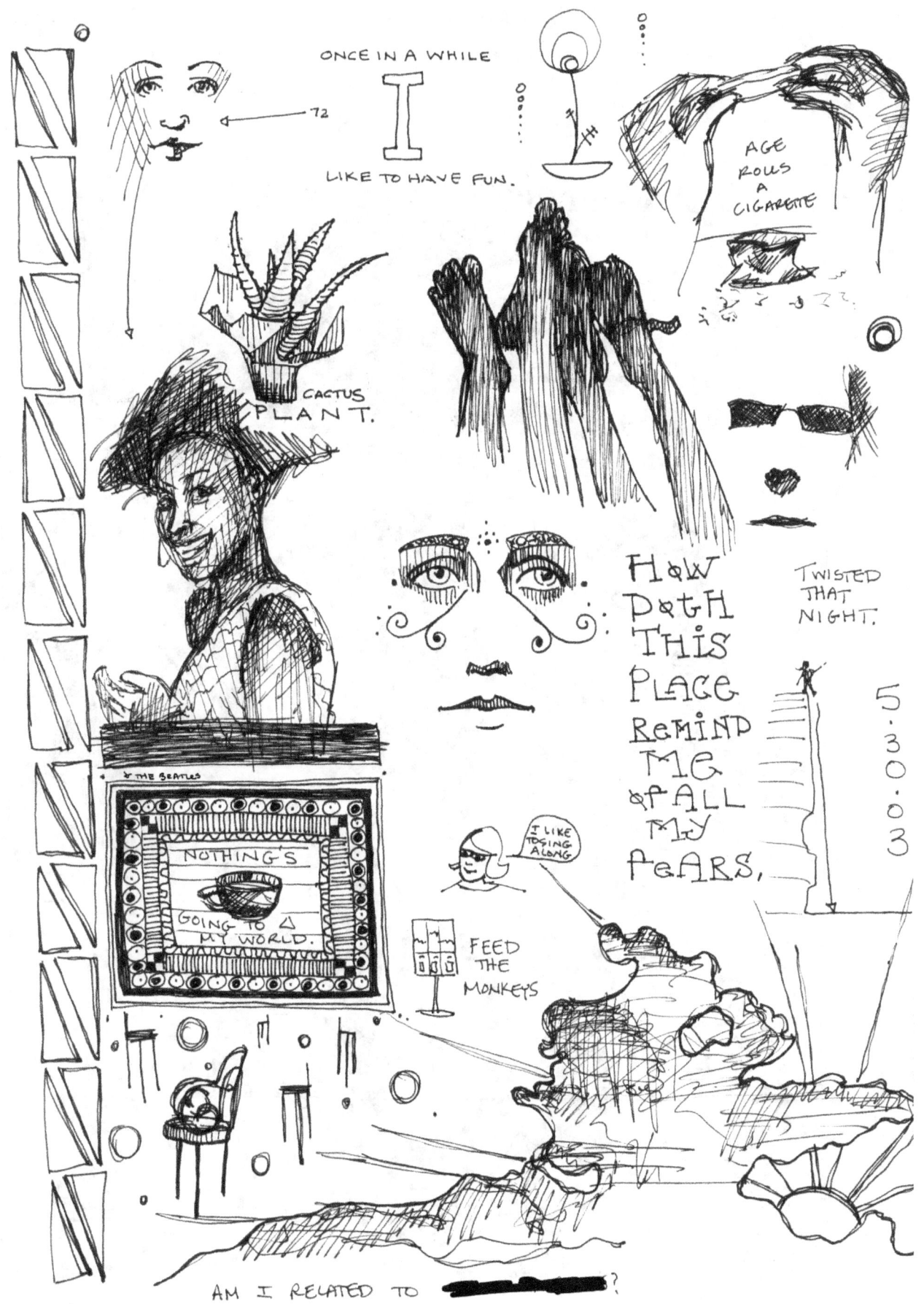

WE'RE NOT GOING TO MAKE IT.

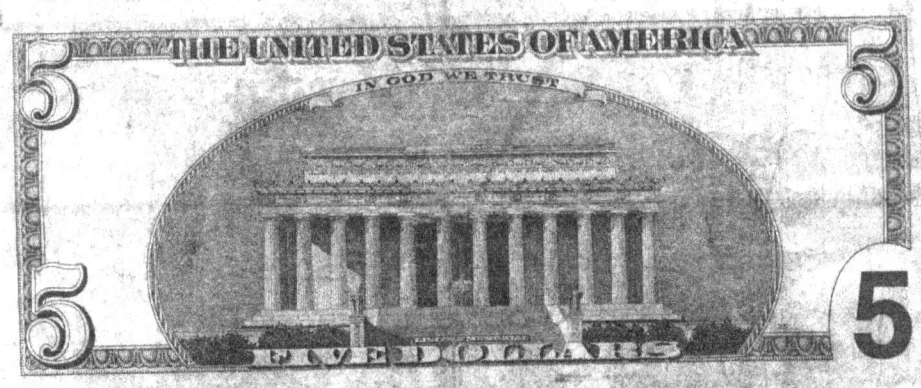

MY PAYMENT FOR DRINKING ONE BEER

A COMPLETE LET DOWN.

NOT REAL

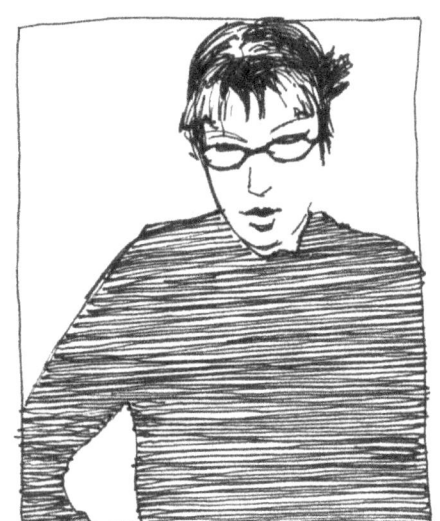

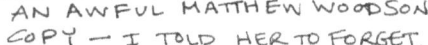

AN AWFUL MATTHEW WOODSON COPY — I TOLD HER TO FORGET.

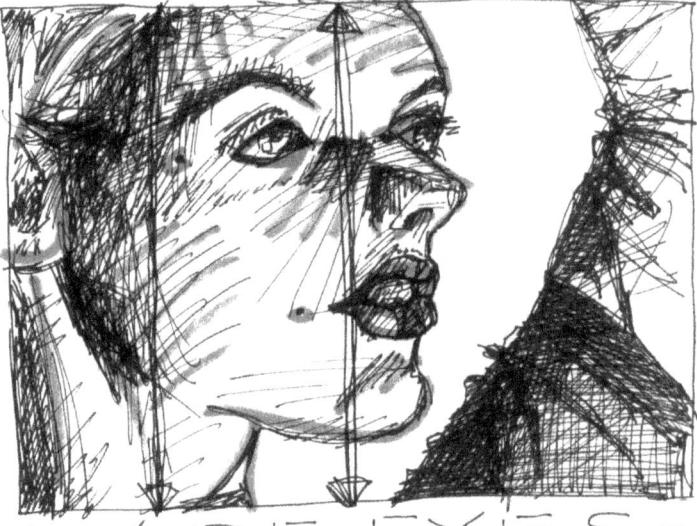

WIDE-EYES-

72"

Once again I am sinking into a sugar-lined pit of my love of love itself. I don't know where I am. I watch myself fade into fog broken by the headlights of your questions. I wonder about you. Violins weep and my eyes roll to the back of my head. I've stopped. I've stopped. Will you kiss me? Will I let you? The daylight fades......

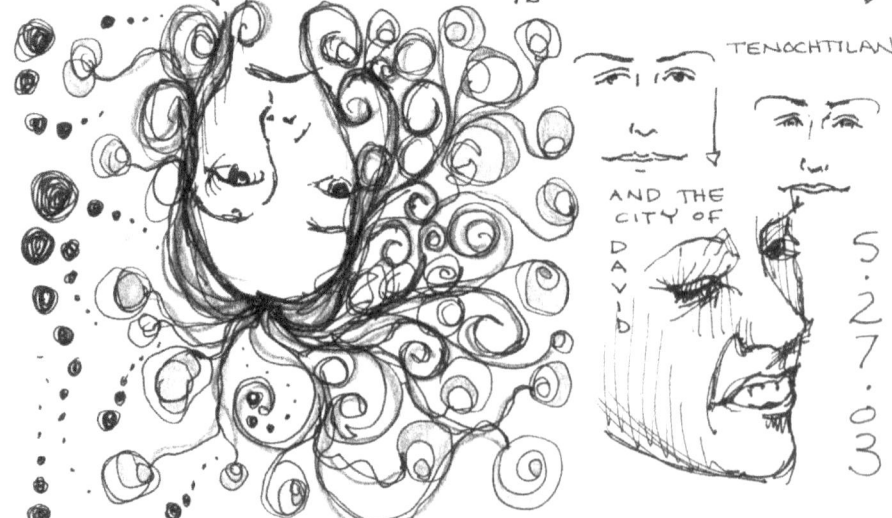

TENOCHTITLAN

AND THE CITY OF DAVID

5.27.03

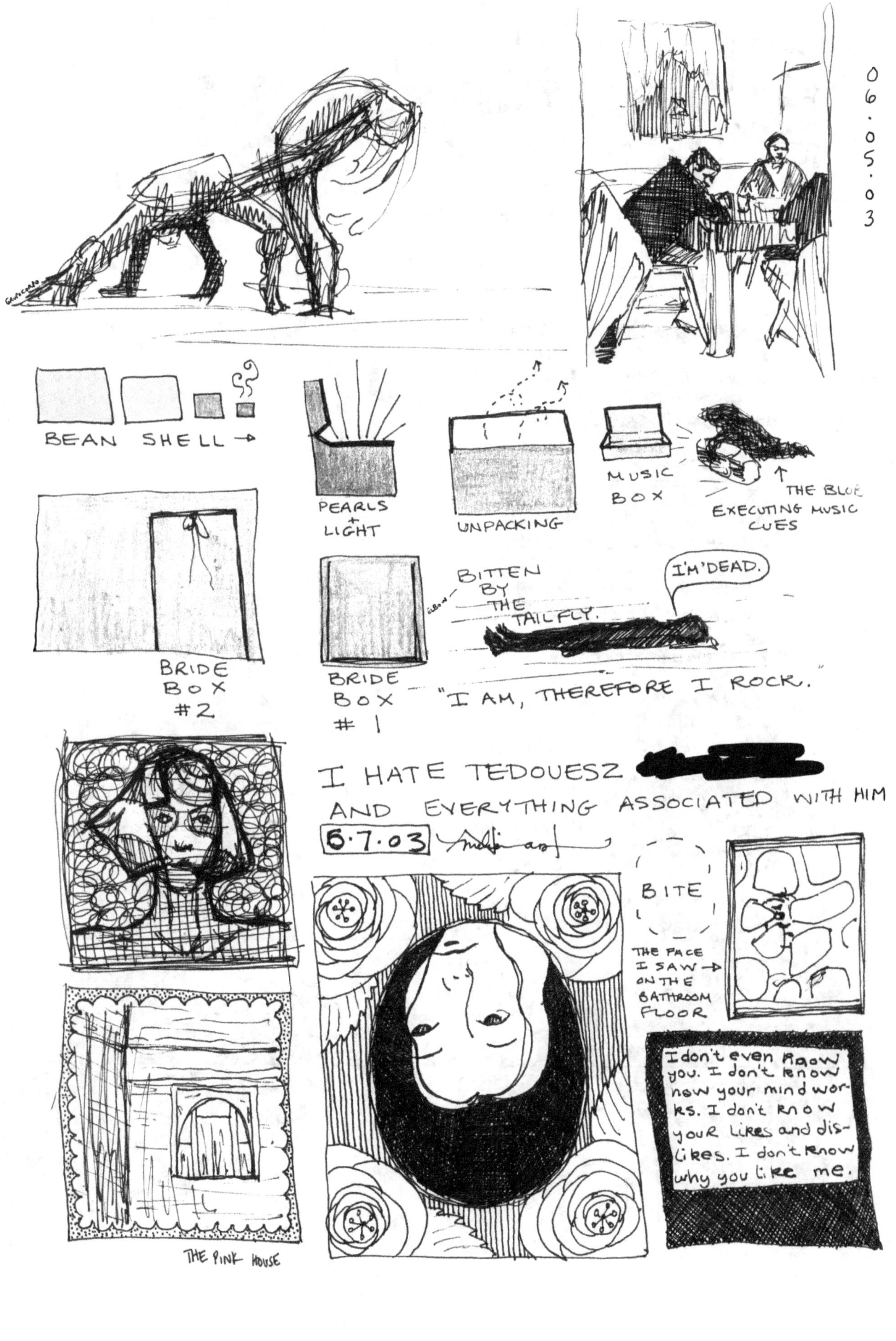

06.05.03

BEAN SHELL →

PEARLS + LIGHT

UNPACKING

MUSIC BOX

THE BLUE EXECUTING MUSIC CUES

BRIDE BOX #2

BRIDE BOX #1

BITTEN BY THE TAIL FLY.

I'M DEAD.

"I AM, THEREFORE I ROCK."

I HATE TEDOUESZ ~~████~~

AND EVERYTHING ASSOCIATED WITH HIM

5·7·03

BITE

THE FACE I SAW → ON THE BATHROOM FLOOR

I don't even know you. I don't know how your mind works. I don't know your likes and dislikes. I don't know why you like me.

THE PINK HOUSE

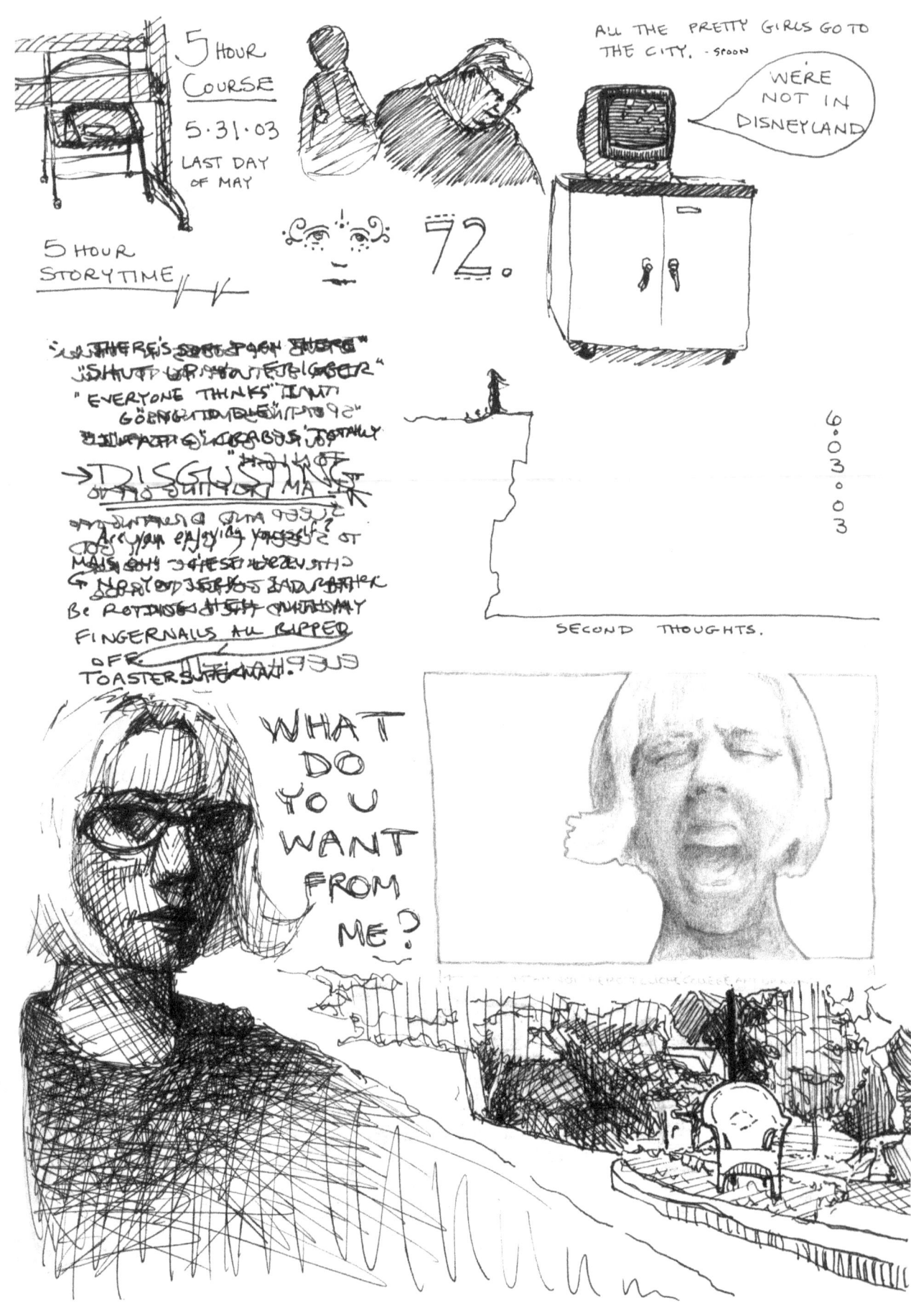

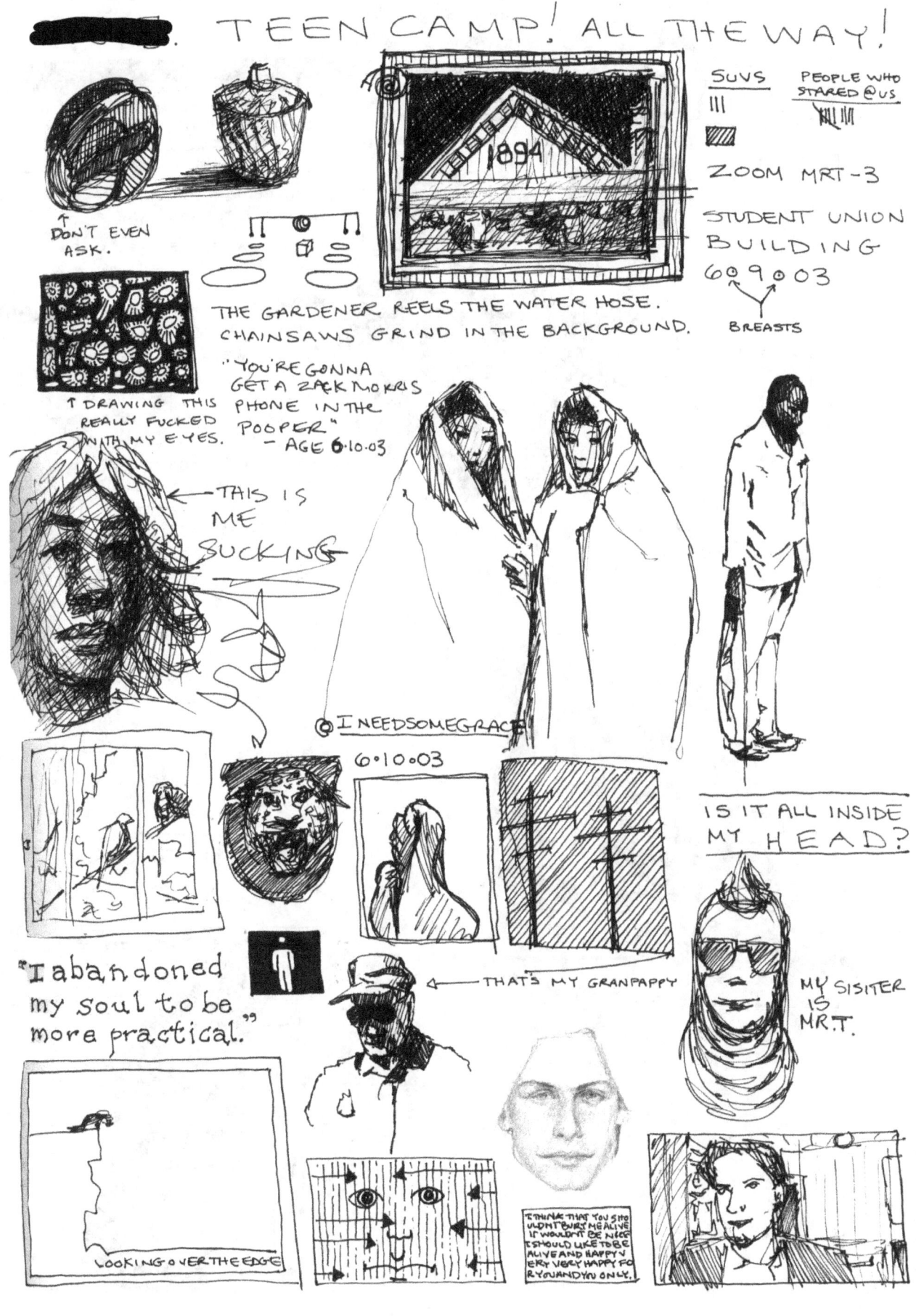

EASE
EA SE
EASE
EASE
EA SE
NO NO
AH YEAH
NO NO
AH YEAH
NO NO
EASE
EASE
EASE

HMMM...

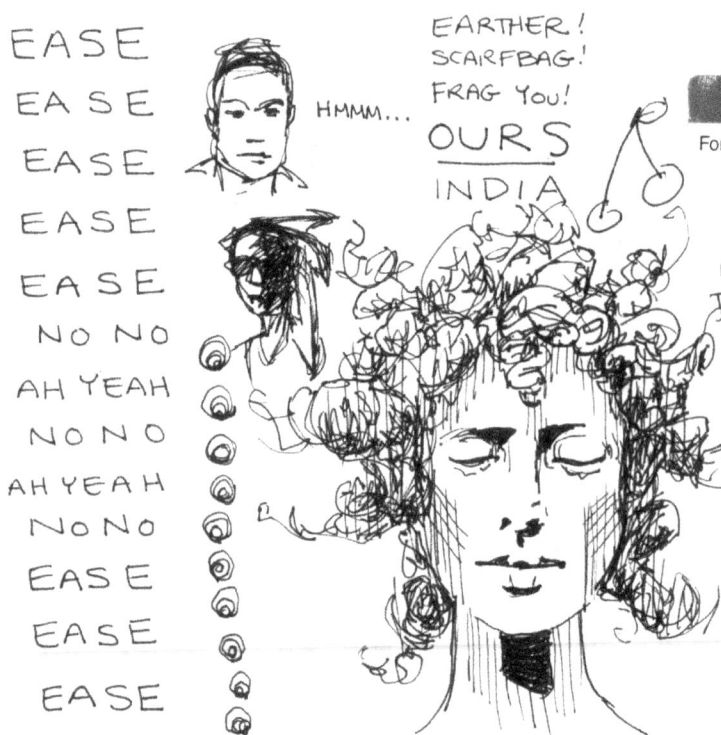

EARTHER!
SCARFBAG!
FRAG YOU!
OURS
INDIA

DO BEES SHIT?

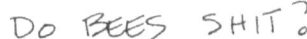

MORE PEOPLE SHOULD WALK DOWN THE STREET HALF-NAKED.

FOUR SETS OF REGULARS BETWEEN 7:30 + 8:00 PM

DAUGHTER KNOCK @ DOOR + WAIT. SHE ANSWERS. THEY CHAT THEN LEAVE.

A LITTLE BOY, SITTING WITH HIS PARENTS THE SECOND TABLE OVER, NOTICES MY SISTER'S MOHAWK AND TRIES TO EXPLAIN IT TO HIS PATIENT FOLKS.

I AM RELATED TO PAUL

WE CREATE BECAUSE THEY DESTROY → DAVID. THERE.

WHEN ROCKS AND STONES START FLYING - I BURY MY HEAD IN MY ARMS.

YOUR DAD IS RICH - AND YOUR MOTHER IS GOING TO DIE. DON'T YOU CRY.

I LIKE HER BETTER AS A CRACK WHORE.

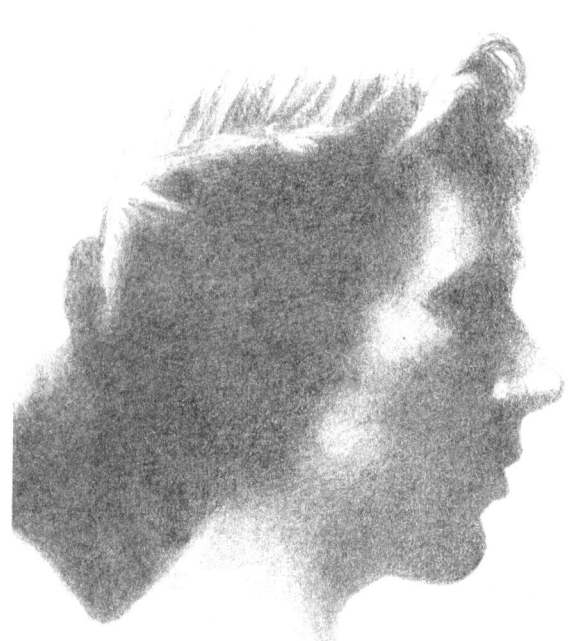

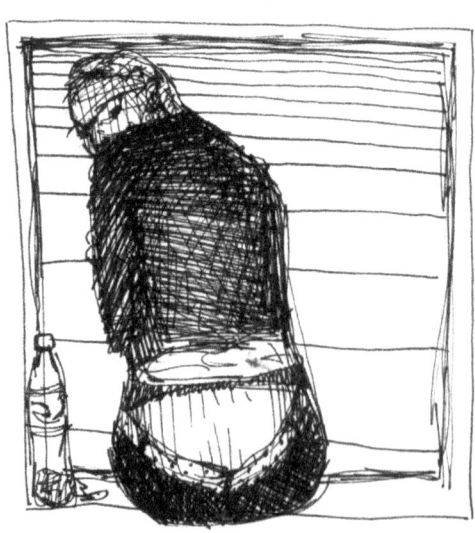

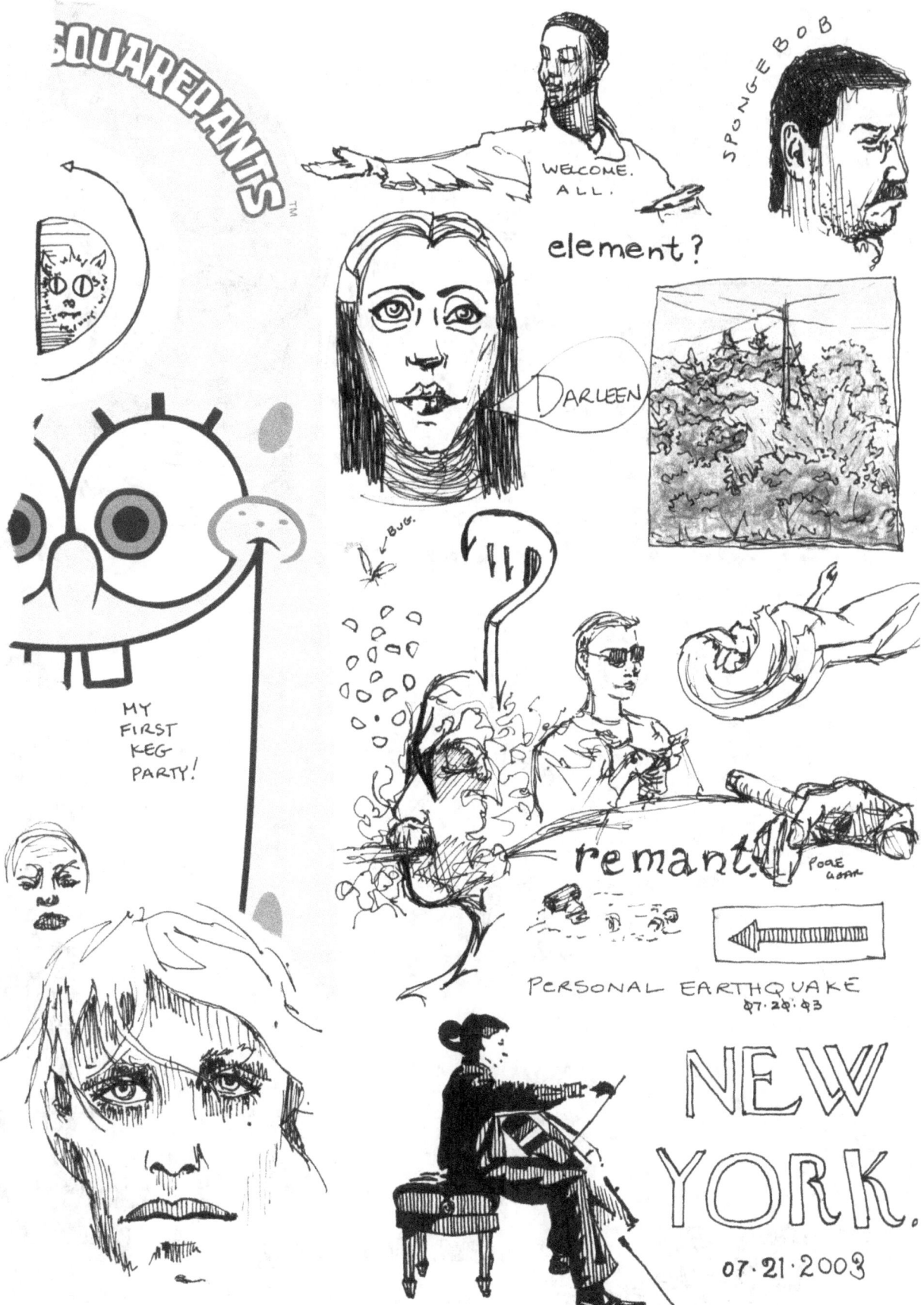

SQUAREPANTS ™

SPONGEBOB

WELCOME.
ALL.

element ?

Darleen

MY
FIRST
KEG
PARTY!

BUG.

remant.

PERSONAL EARTHQUAKE
07·20·93

NEW
YORK.

07·21·2003

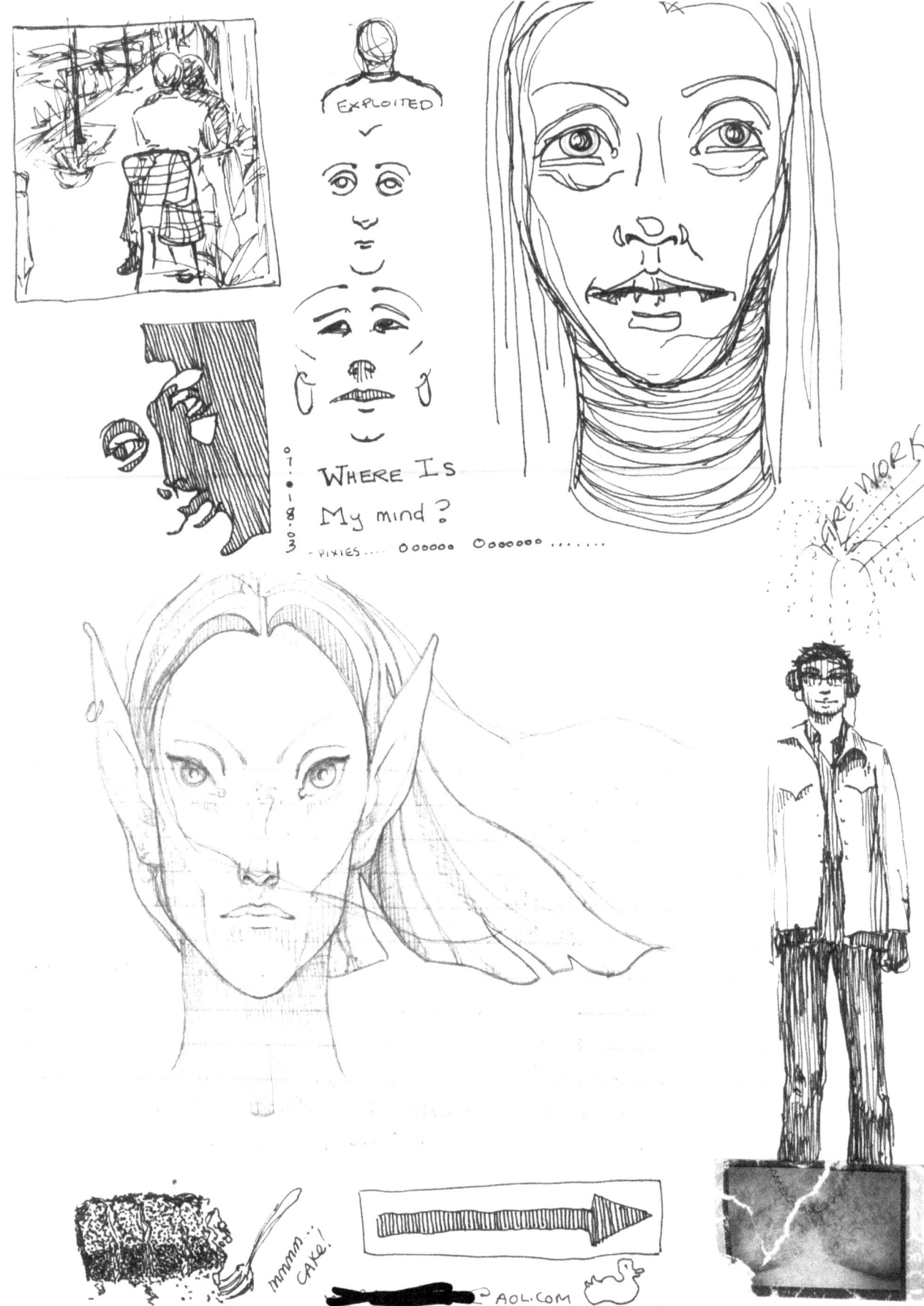

EXPLOITED

07·08·03

WHERE IS
My mind?
- PIXIES.... Ooooooo Ooooooo ....

FIREWORK

mmmm... CAKE!

AOL.COM

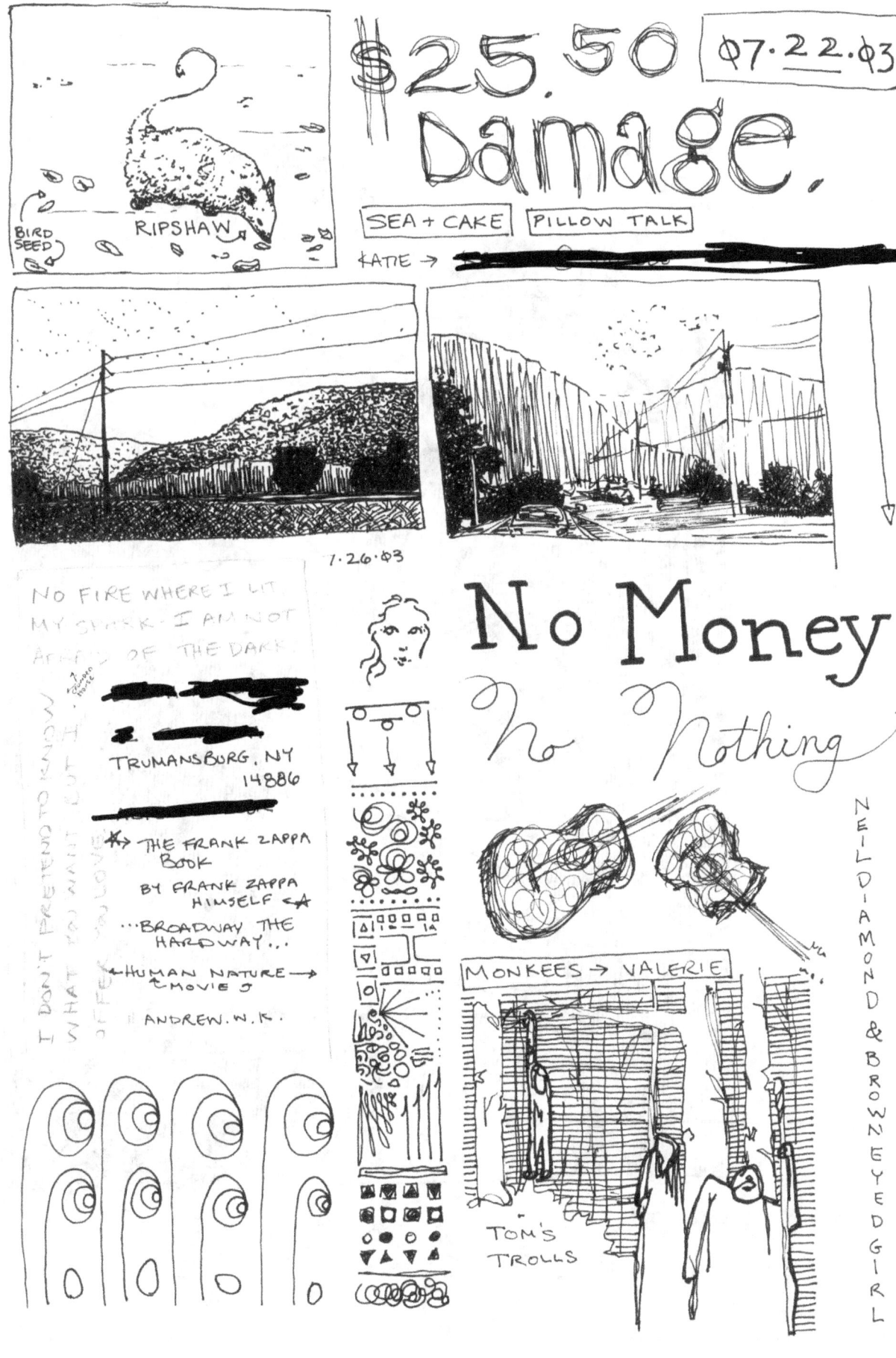

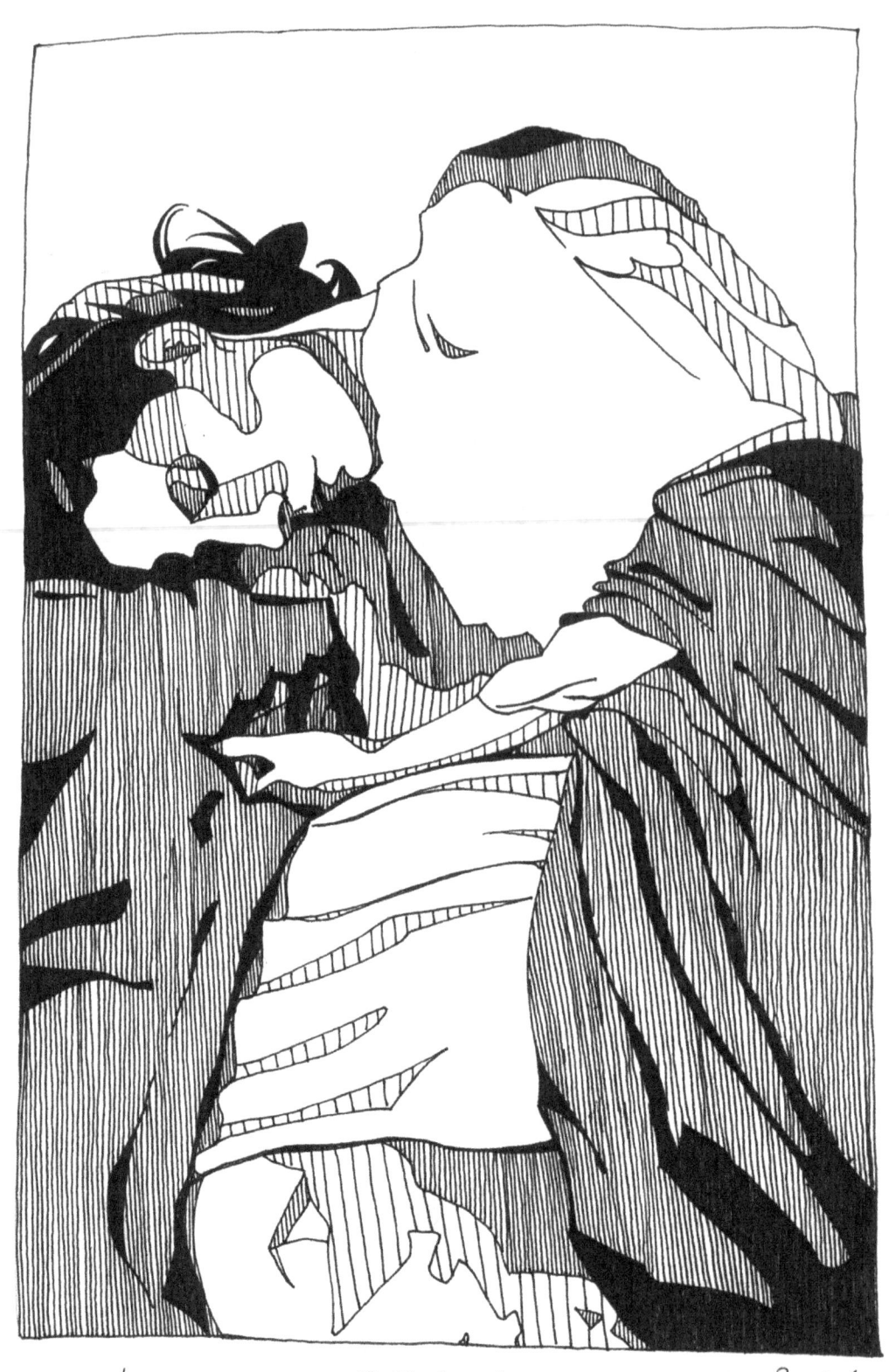

SO THAT'S IT. I BEGIN TO FALL & YOU
ROLL OUT FIRST. SMART MOVE.

7·24·03
7·22·03

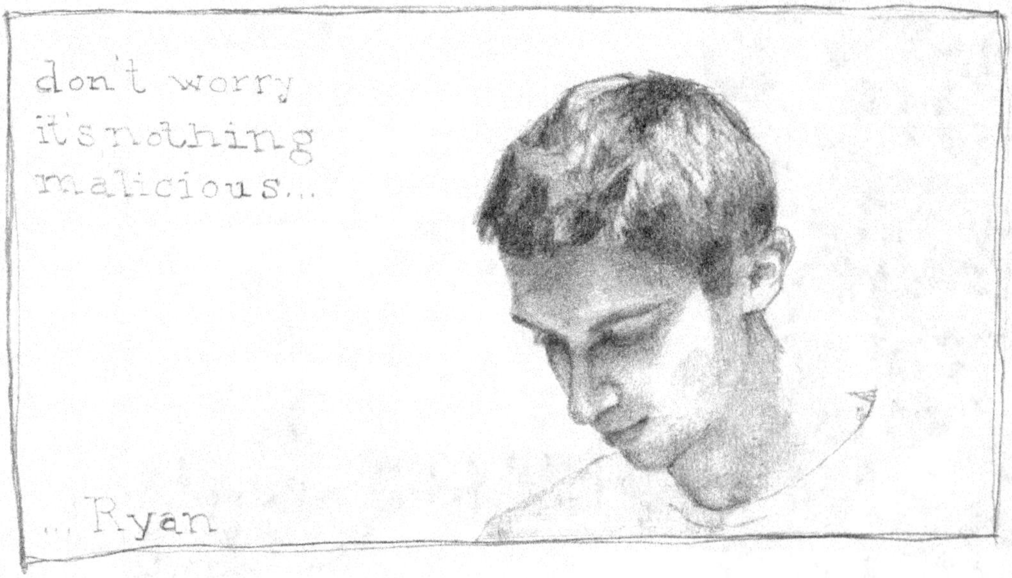
don't worry
it's nothing
malicious...
...Ryan

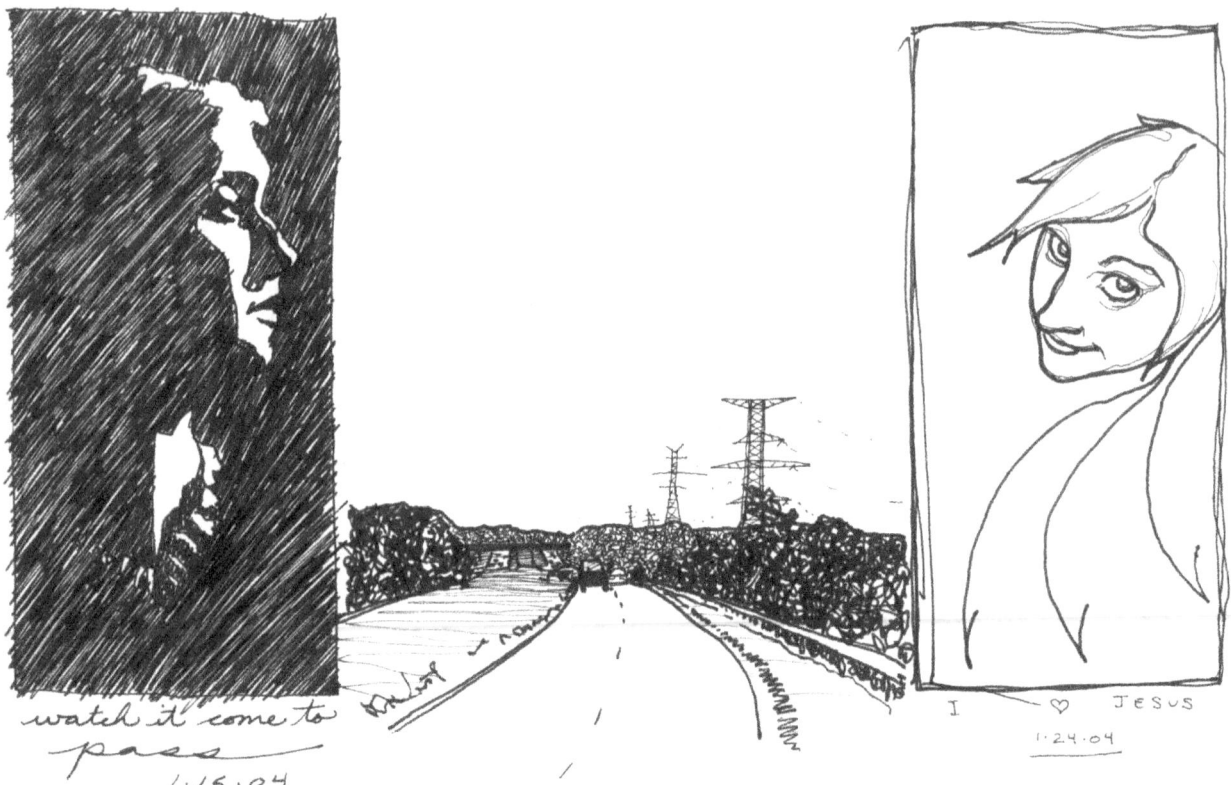

watch it come to *pass* 1.15.04

I ♡ JESUS
1·24·04

warm light on a winter's day

everything's blue and gold - the sun that comes through my window -
my hair, and my eyes, and my skin. let everything just sink in - and i know....

GENIUNE PEOPLE 1·24·04

the muse 1·24·04

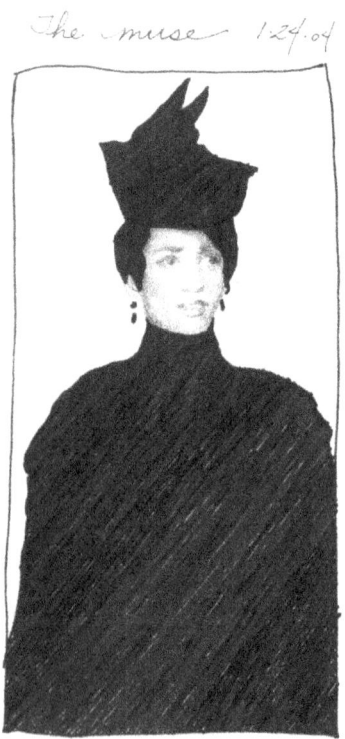

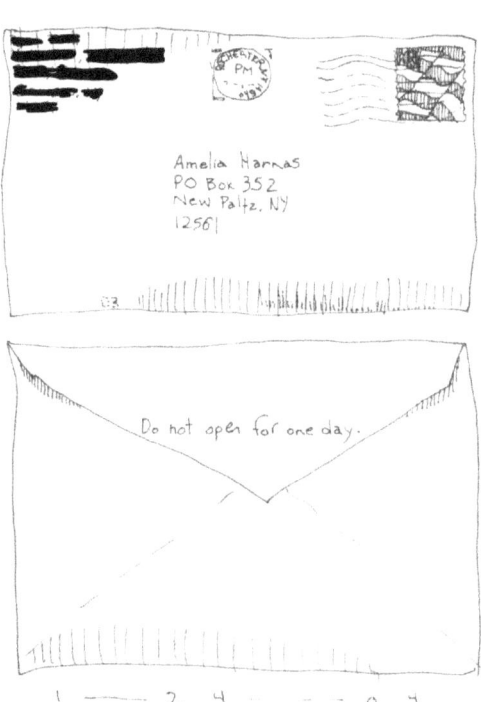

Amelia Harnas
PO Box 352
New Paltz, NY
12561

Do not open for one day.

1 — 2 4 - - 0 4

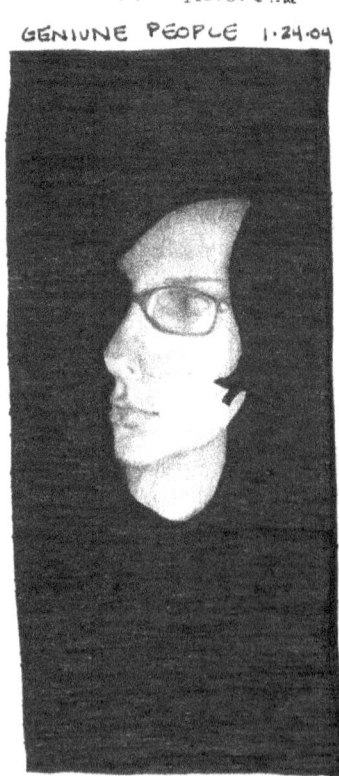

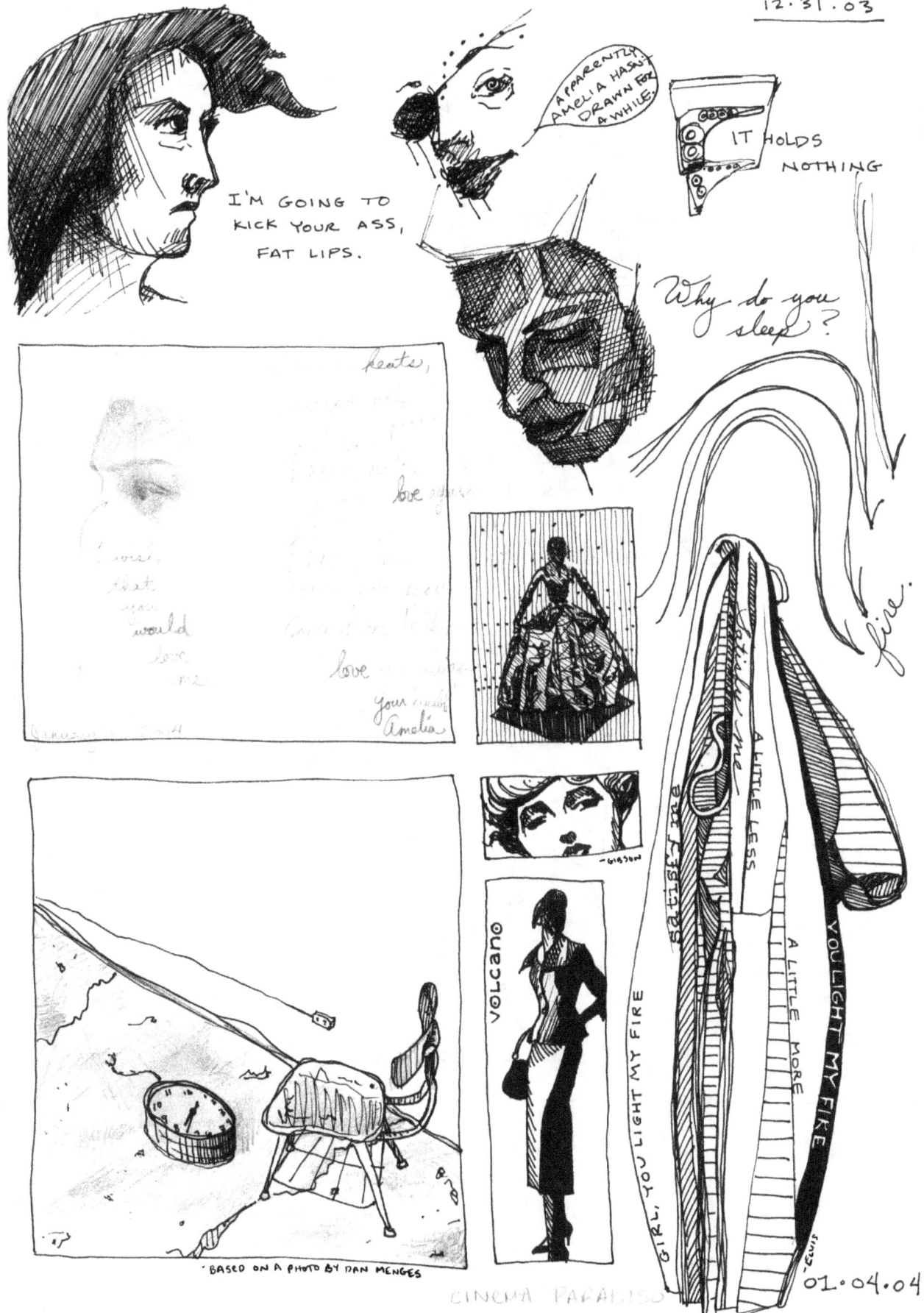

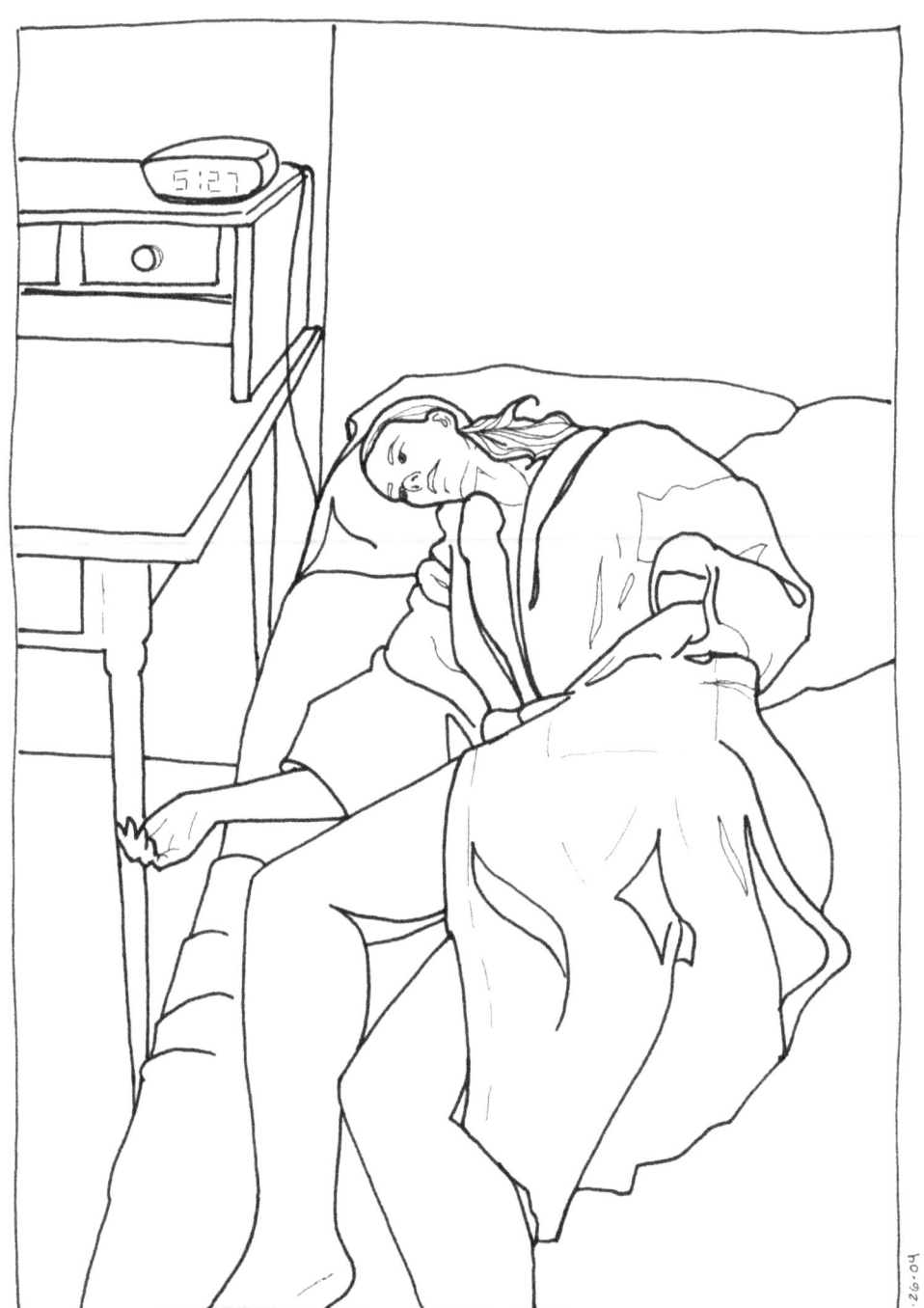

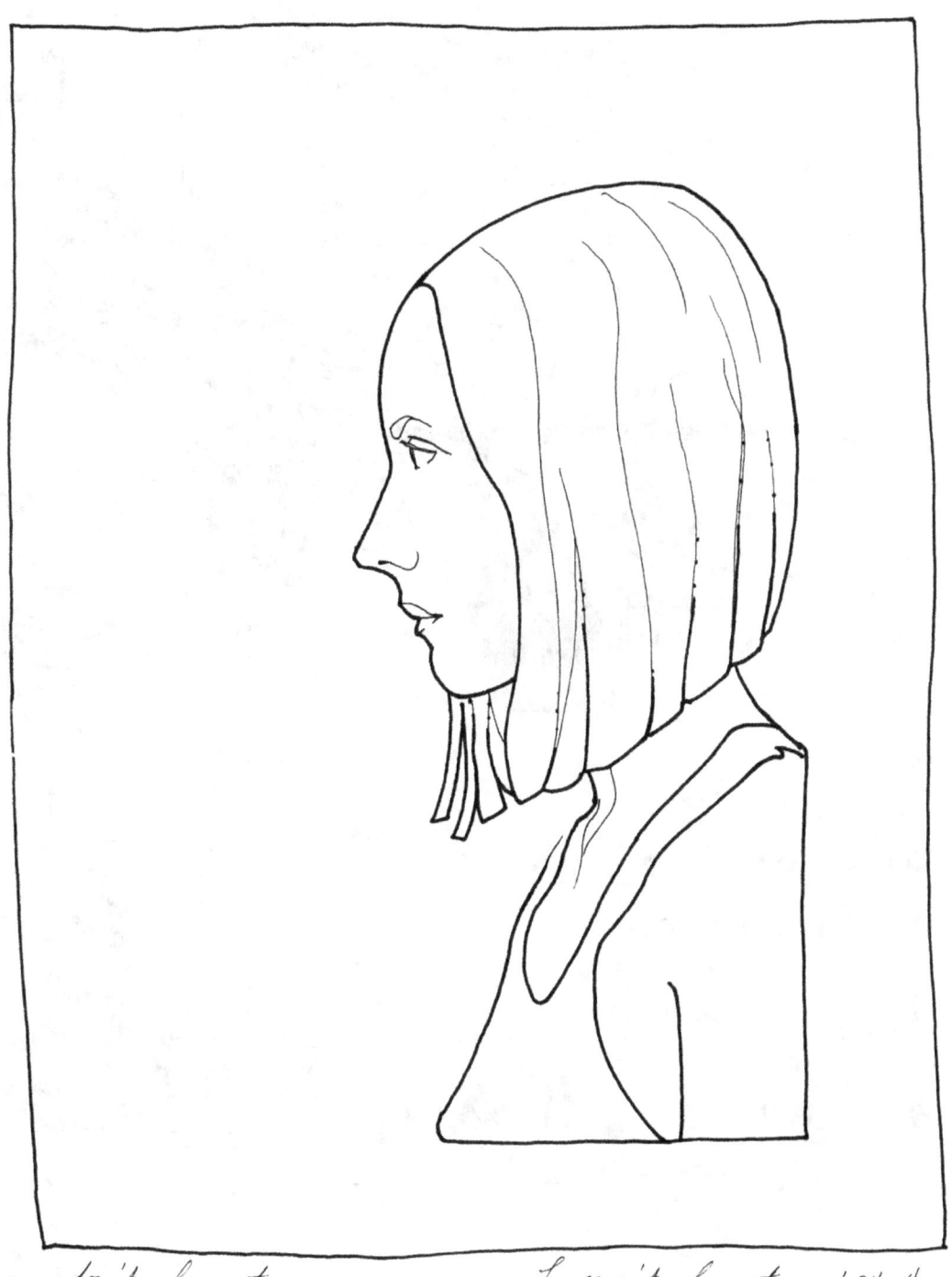

don't forget. ——————————— I can't forget.   1·24·04

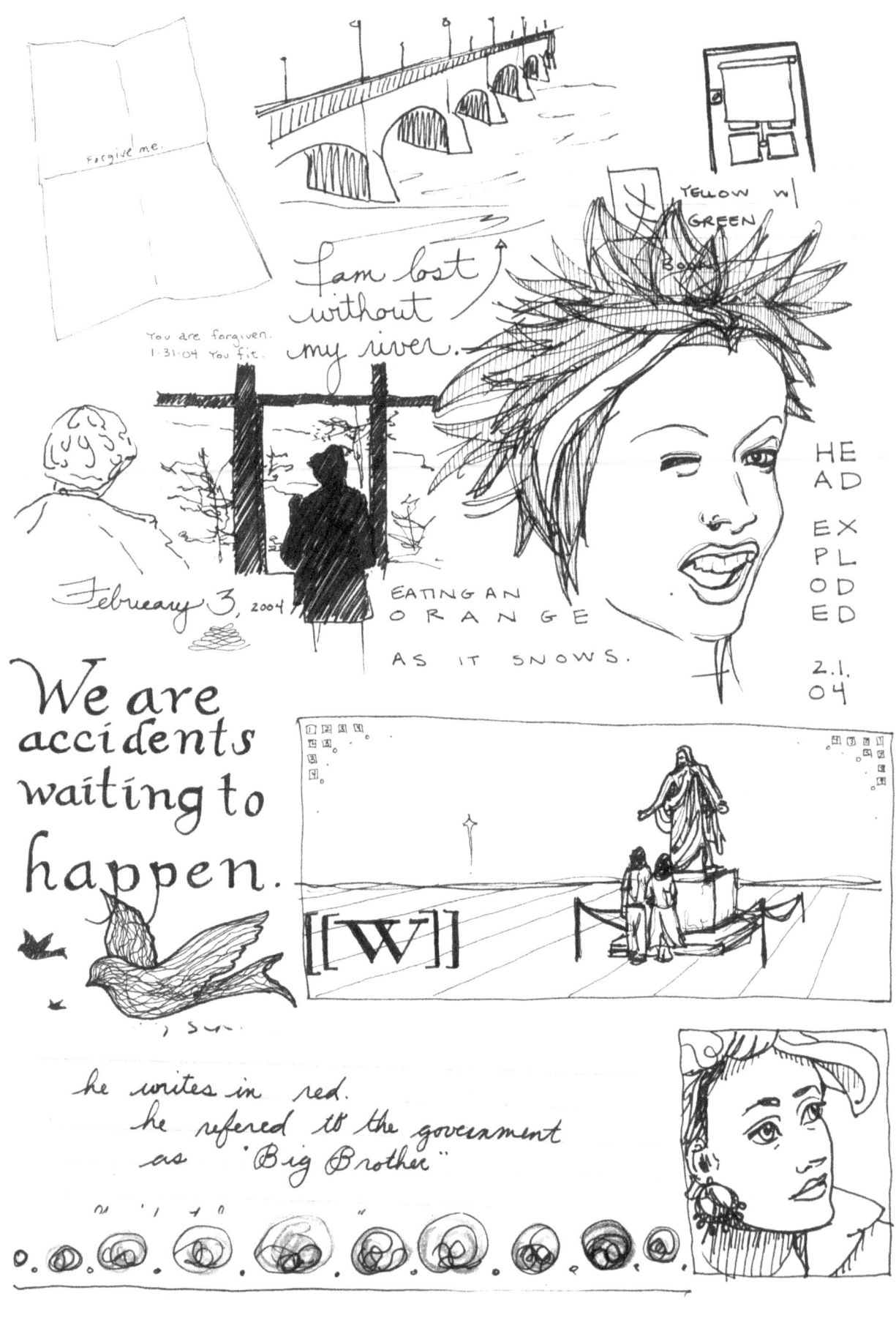

Forgive me.

I am lost without my river.

You are forgiven.
1·31·04 You fit.

YELLOW W/ GREEN

February 3, 2004

EATING AN
ORANGE

AS IT SNOWS.

HE
AD
EX
PL
O
D
ED

2.1.
04

We are
accidents
waiting to
happen.

[[W]]

he writes in red.
he refered to the government
as "Big Brother"

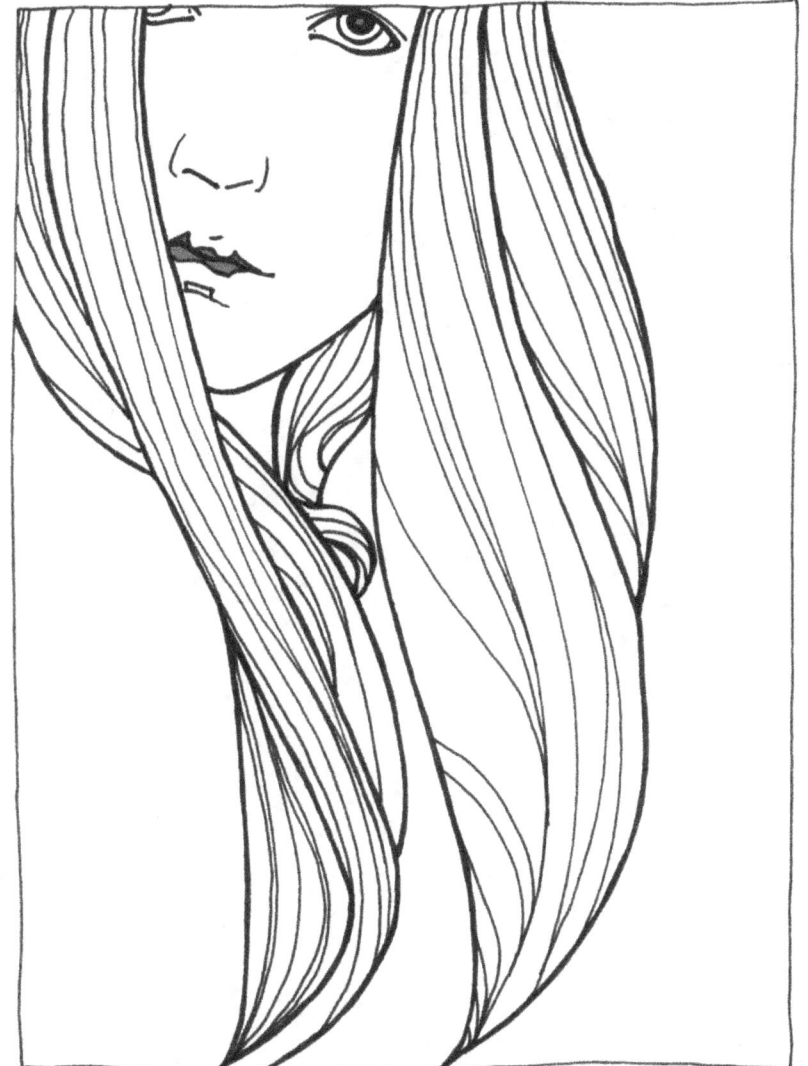

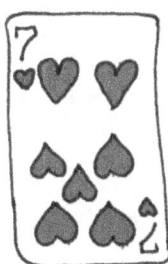

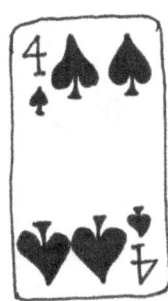

40 The Warning Waits Suspect. 2

- I MESSED UP THE QUOTE BY DAVID IVANICK

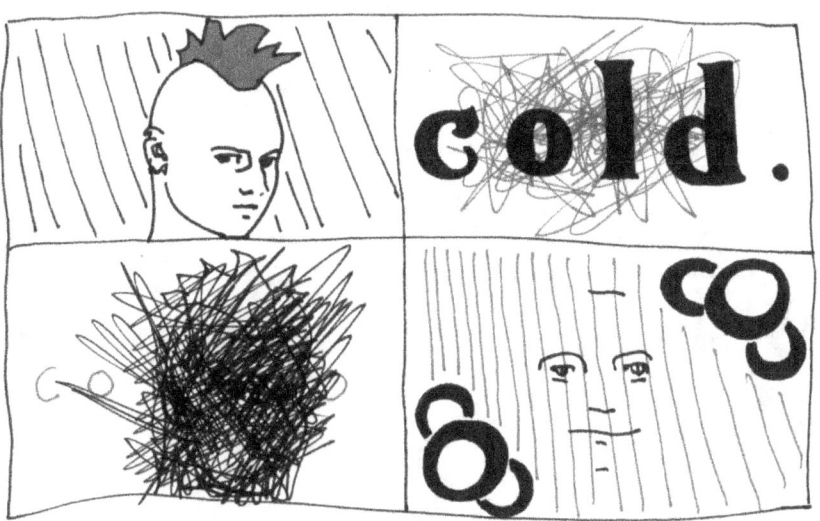

4 cards chosen
at random.

Luck.

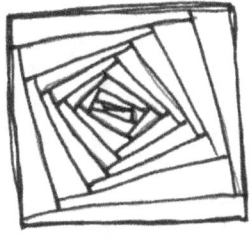

3.24.04.

My dear Jenny

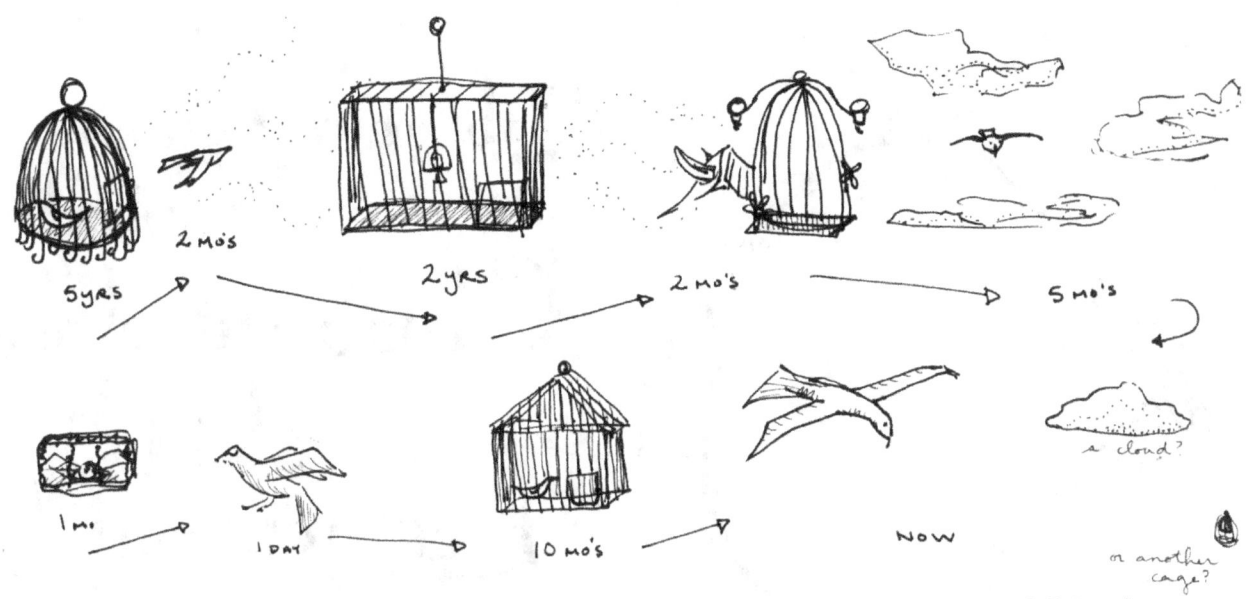

I'd tell you that I love you, but I'm sorry - I'm sorry... it's already been said.

7.27.04

— ADAM LINDQVIST

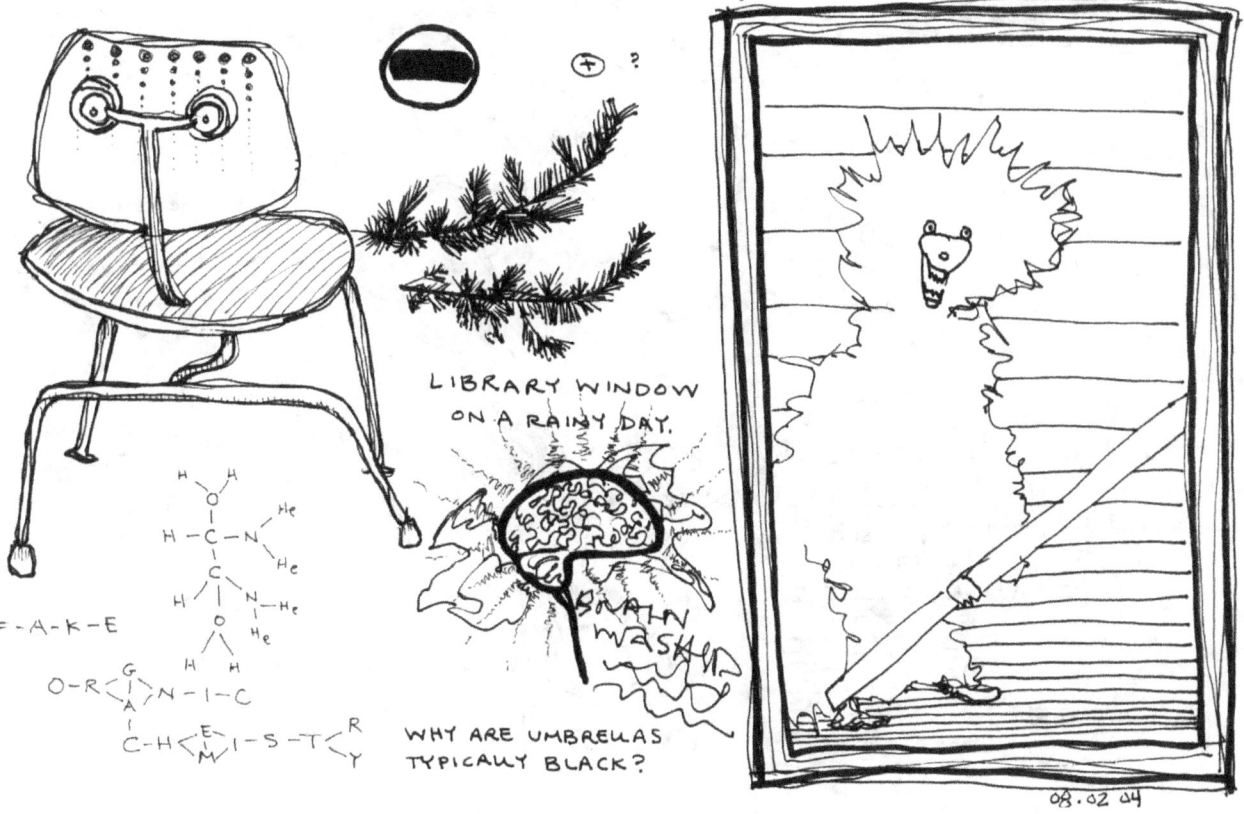

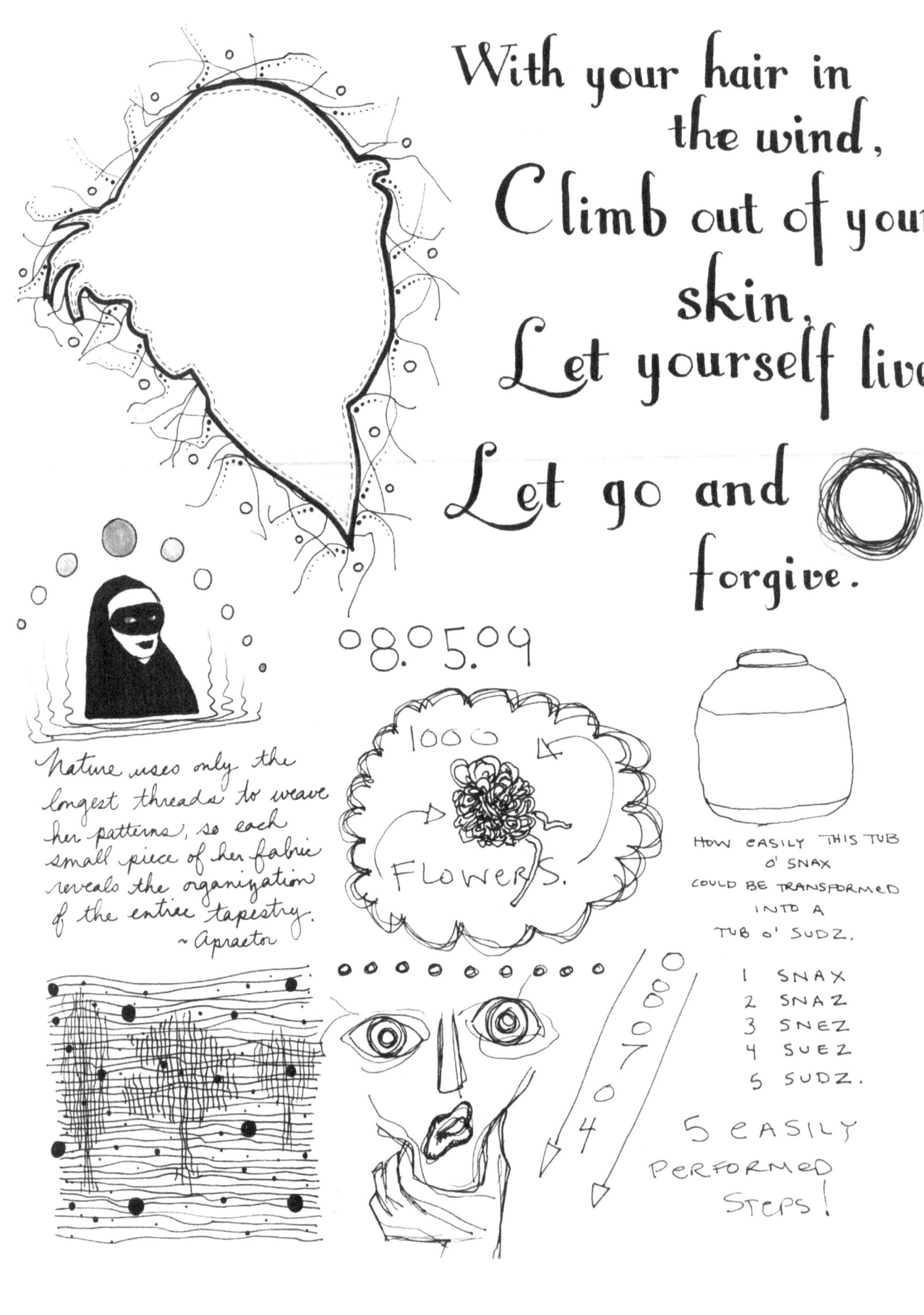

With your hair in
the wind,
Climb out of your
skin,
Let yourself live.

Let go and
forgive.

08.05.09

Nature uses only the
longest threads to weave
her patterns, so each
small piece of her fabric
reveals the organization
of the entire tapestry.
~ Apraetor

1000
FLOWERS.

HOW EASILY THIS TUB
O' SNAX
COULD BE TRANSFORMED
INTO A
TUB O' SUDZ.

1 SNAX
2 SNAZ
3 SNEZ
4 SUEZ
5 SUDZ.

5 EASILY
PERFORMED
STEPS!

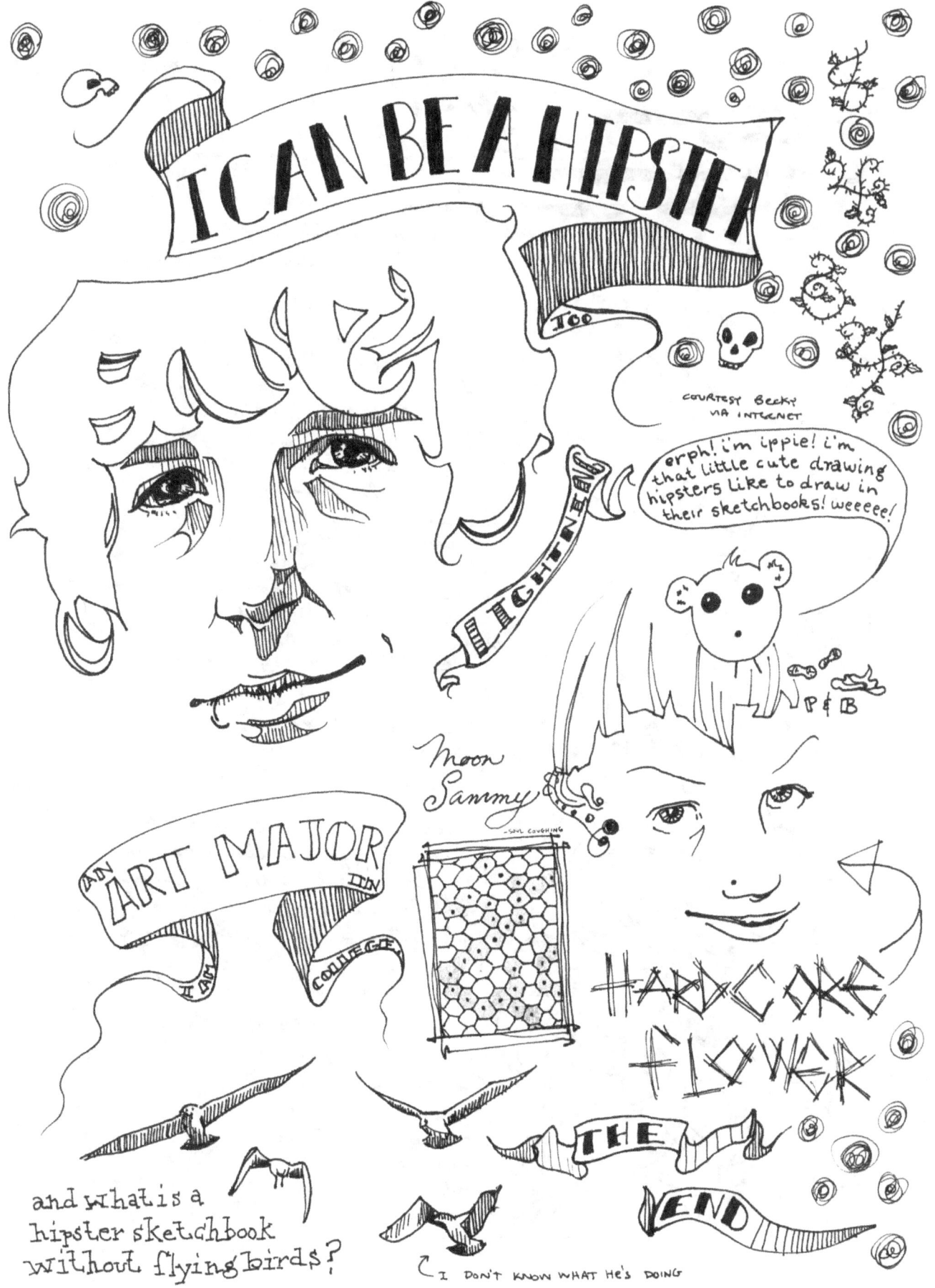

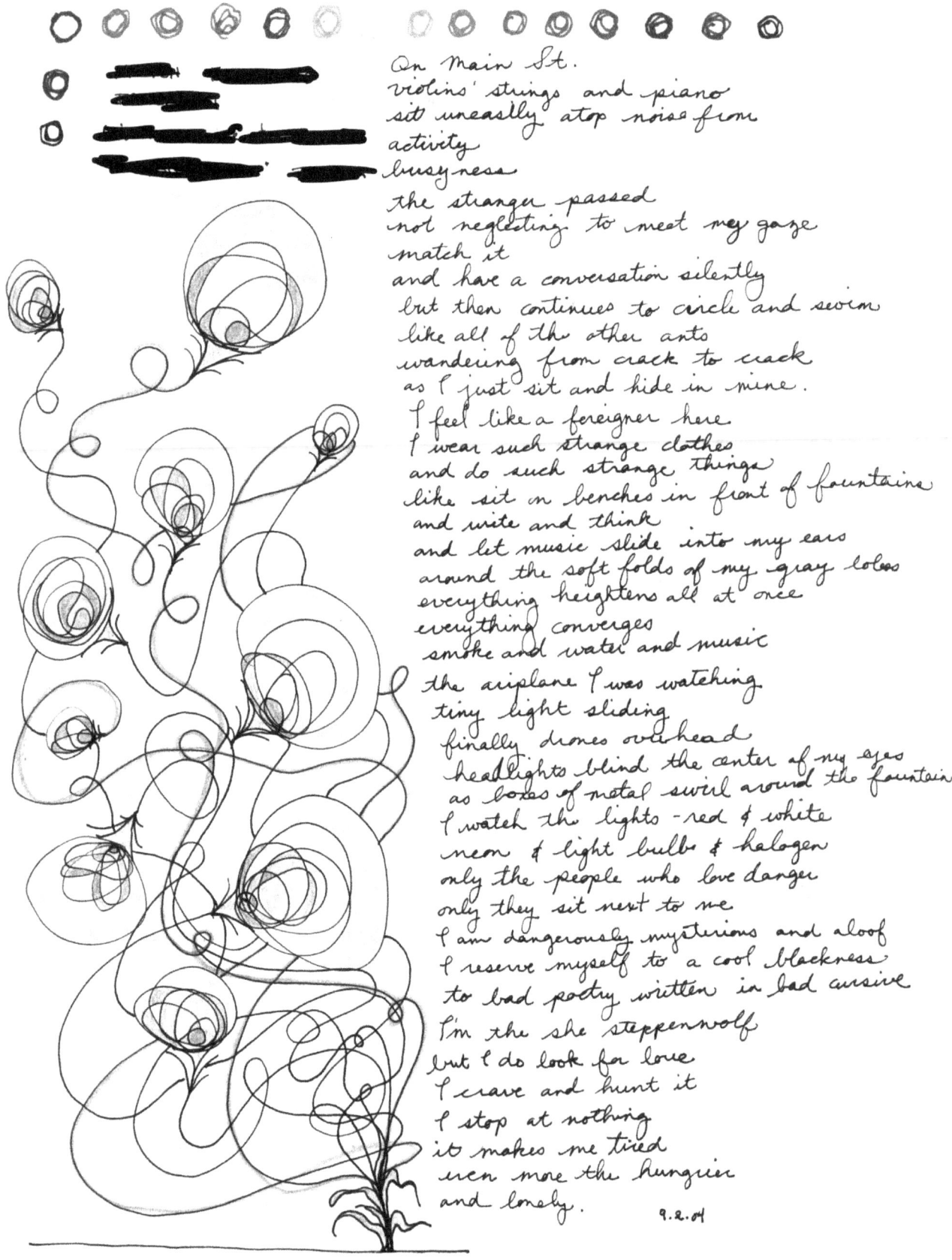

On Main St.
violins' strings and piano
sit uneasily atop noise from
activity
busyness
the stranger passed
not neglecting to meet my gaze
match it
and have a conversation silently
but then continues to circle and swim
like all of the other ants
wandering from crack to crack
as I just sit and hide in mine.
I feel like a foreigner here
I wear such strange clothes
and do such strange things
like sit on benches in front of fountains
and write and think
and let music slide into my ears
around the soft folds of my gray lobes
everything heightens all at once
everything converges
smoke and water and music
the airplane I was watching
tiny light sliding
finally drones overhead
headlights blind the center of my eyes
as boxes of metal swirl around the fountain
I watch the lights - red & white
neon & light bulbs & halogen
only the people who love danger
only they sit next to me
I am dangerously mysterious and aloof
I reserve myself to a cool blackness
to bad poetry written in bad cursive
I'm the she steppenwolf
but I do look for love
I crave and hunt it
I stop at nothing
it makes me tired
even more the hungrier
and lonely.
                    9.2.04

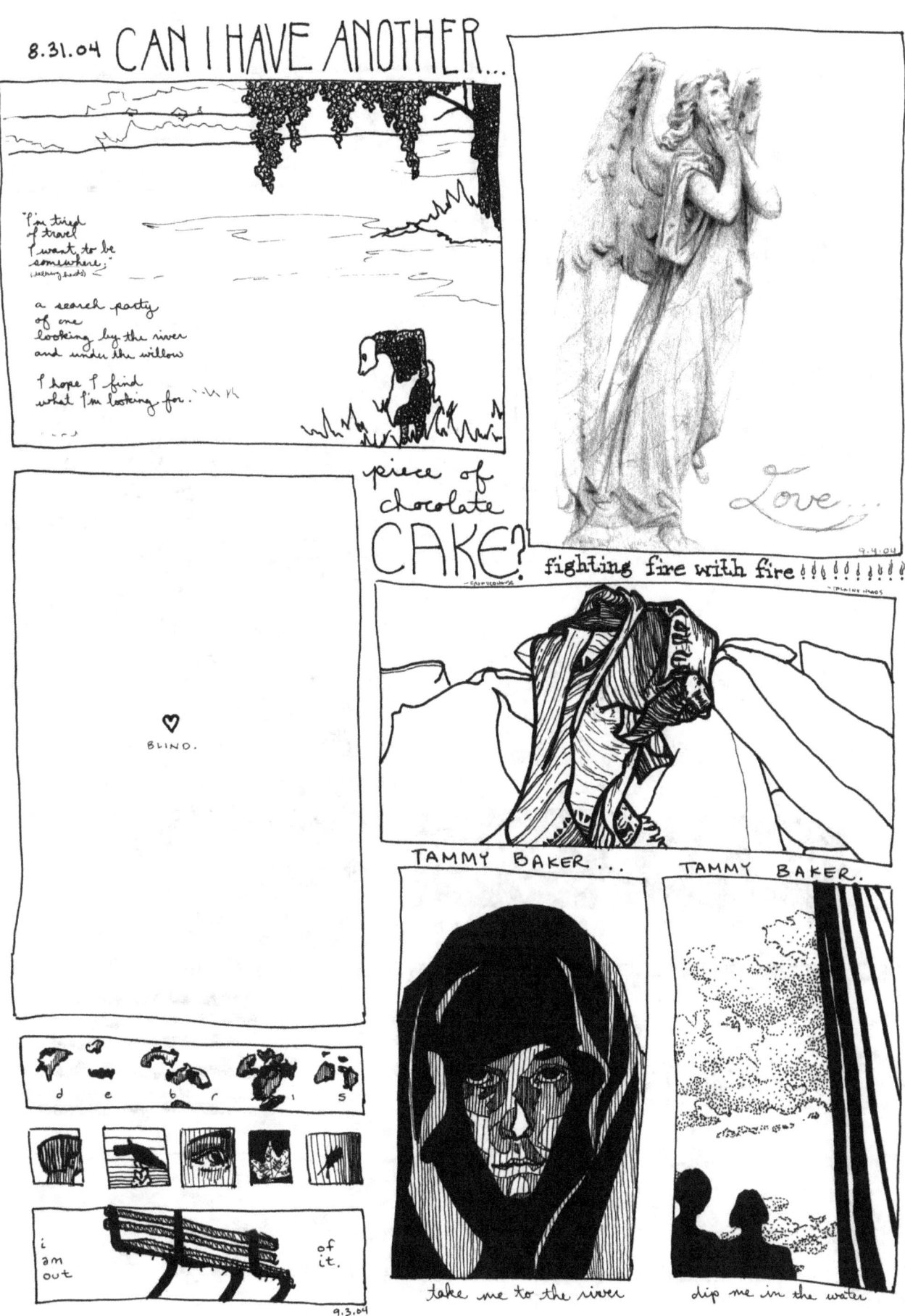

8.31.04 CAN I HAVE ANOTHER...

"I'm tired
of travel
I want to be
somewhere;"
(memory loads)

a search party
of one
looking by the river
and under the willow

I hope I find
what I'm looking for.

piece of
chocolate
CAKE?

Love...

9.4.04

♡

BLIND.

fighting fire with fire!!!!!!!!!!

TAMMY BAKER...   TAMMY BAKER.

d e b r i s

i
am
out

of
it.

9.3.04

take me to the river   dip me in the water

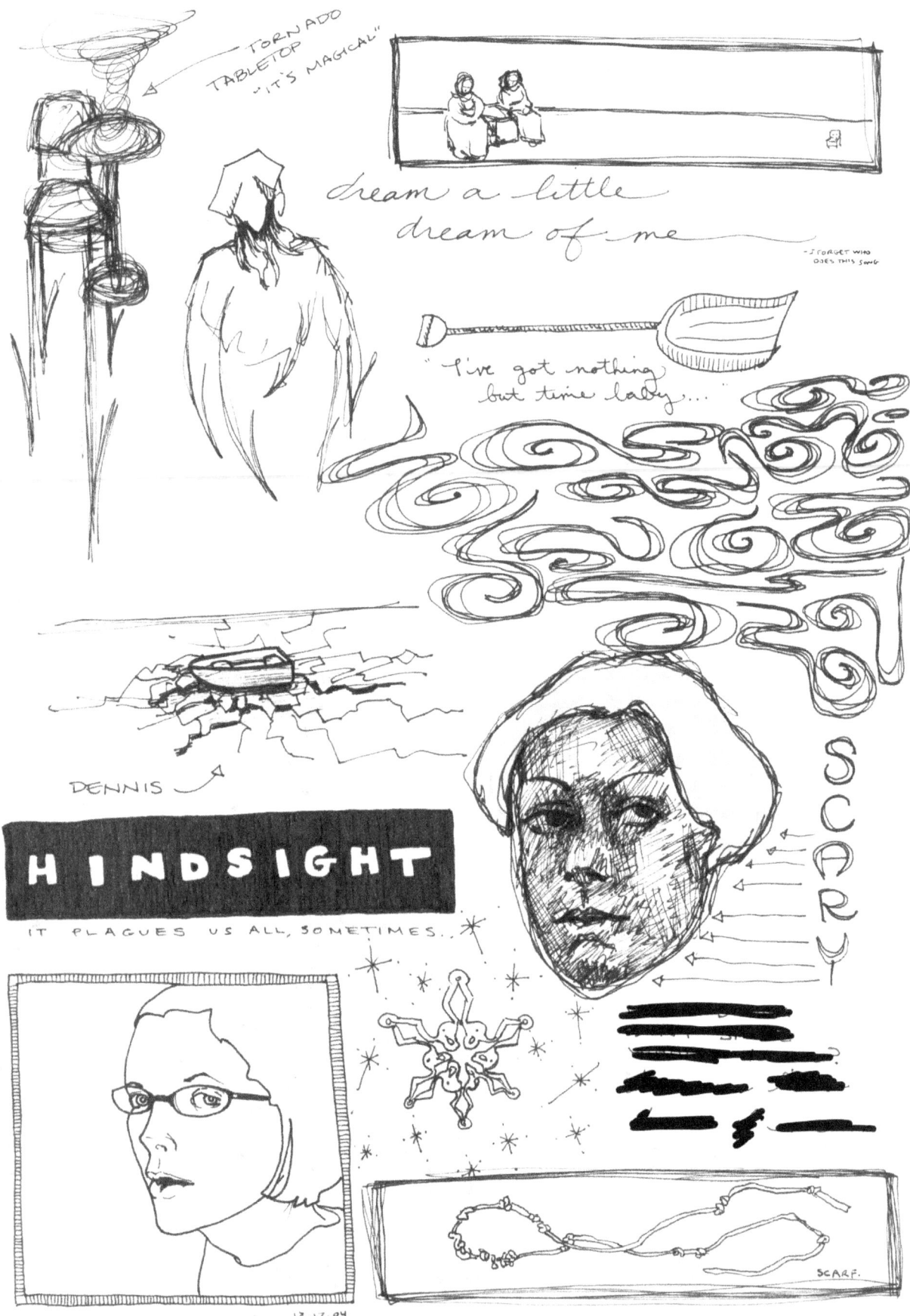

TORNADO TABLETOP "IT'S MAGICAL"

dream a little
dream of me

- I FORGET WHO
DOES THIS SONG

"I've got nothing
but time lady..."

DENNIS

HINDSIGHT

IT PLAGUES US ALL, SOMETIMES..

SCARY

SCARF.

12.17.04

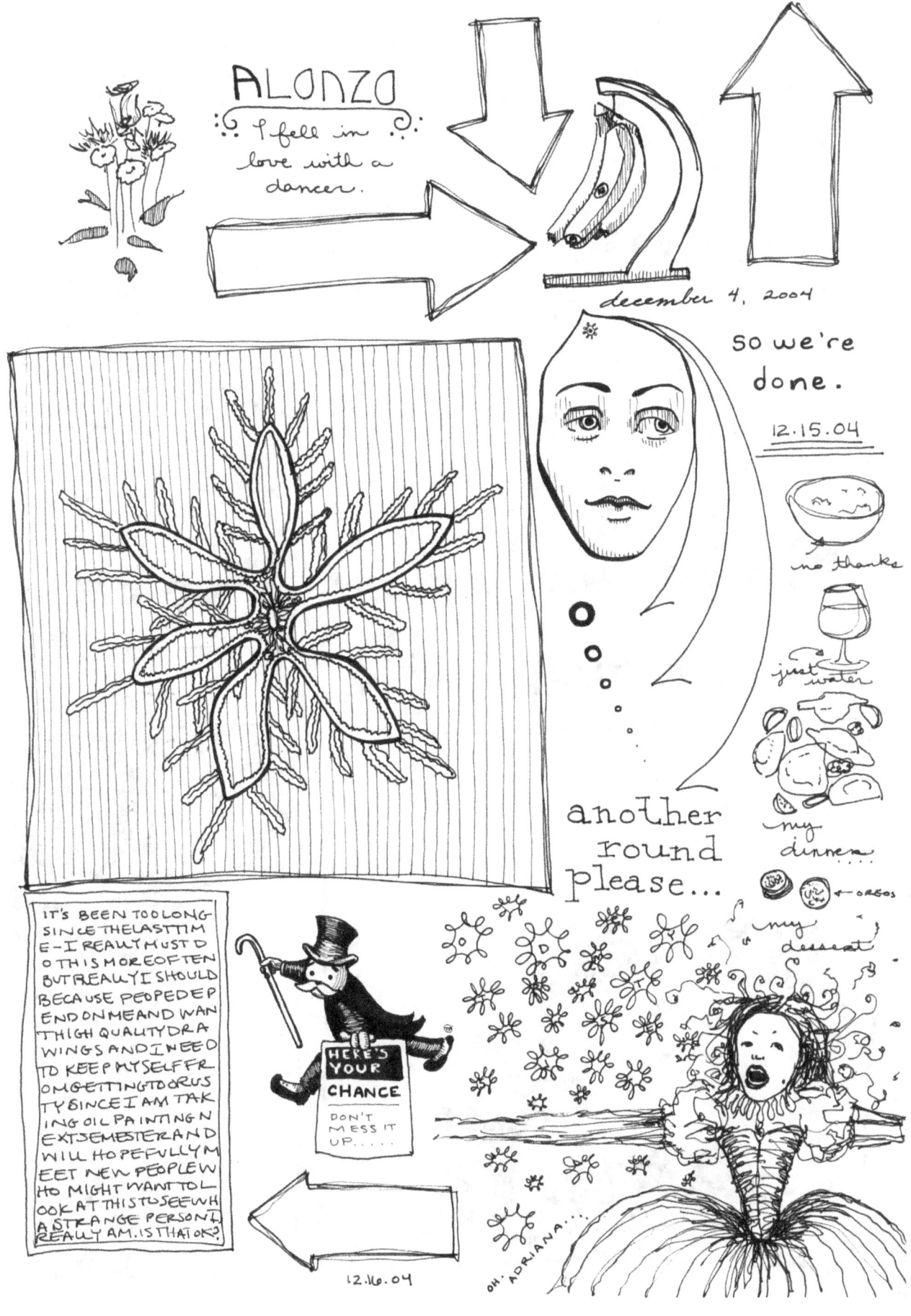

ALONZO
: I fell in love with a dancer.

december 4, 2004

so we're done.

12.15.04

no thanks

just water

my dinner

← OREOS

my dessert

another round please...

IT'S BEEN TOO LONG SINCE THE LAST TIME - I REALLY MUST DO THIS MORE OFTEN BUT REALLY I SHOULD BECAUSE PEOPLE DEPEND ON ME AND WANT HIGH QUALITY DRAWINGS AND I NEED TO KEEP MYSELF FROM GETTING TOO RUSTY SINCE I AM TAKING OIL PAINTING NEXT SEMESTER AND WILL HOPEFULLY MEET NEW PEOPLE WHO MIGHT WANT TO LOOK AT THIS TO SEE WHAT A STRANGE PERSON I REALLY AM. IS THAT OK?

HERE'S YOUR CHANCE
DON'T MESS IT UP.....

12.16.04

OH. ADRIANA...

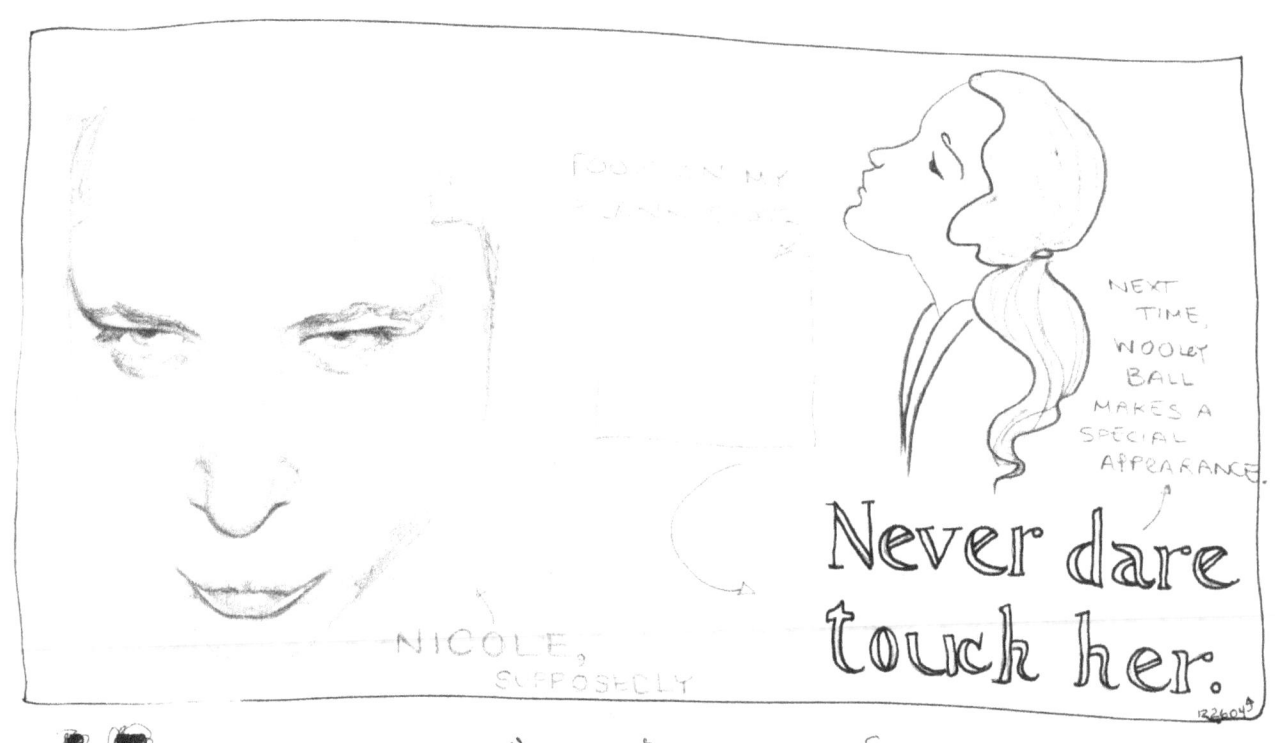

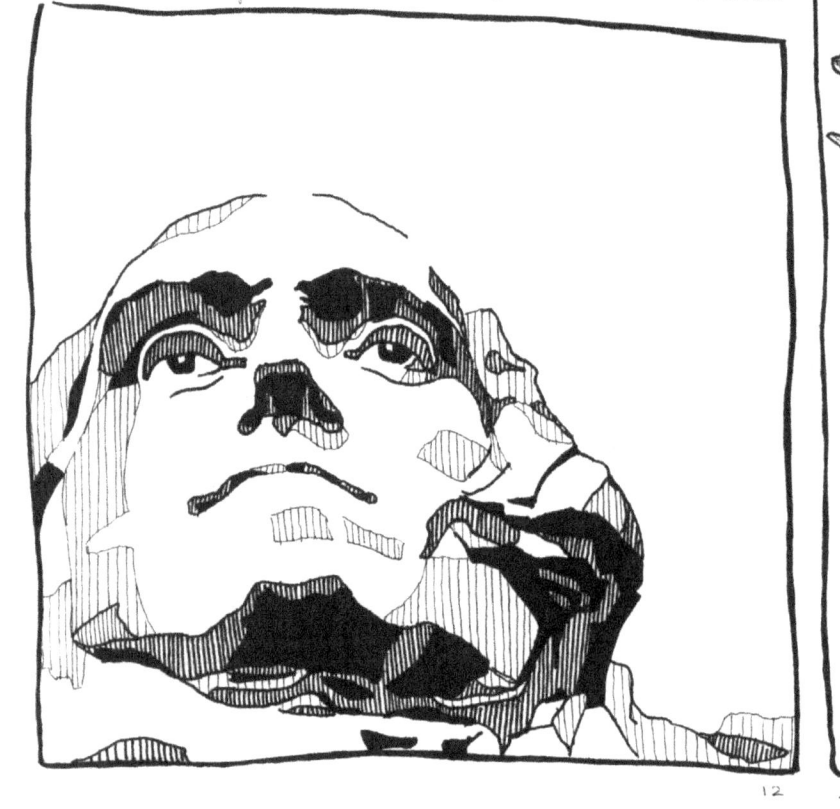
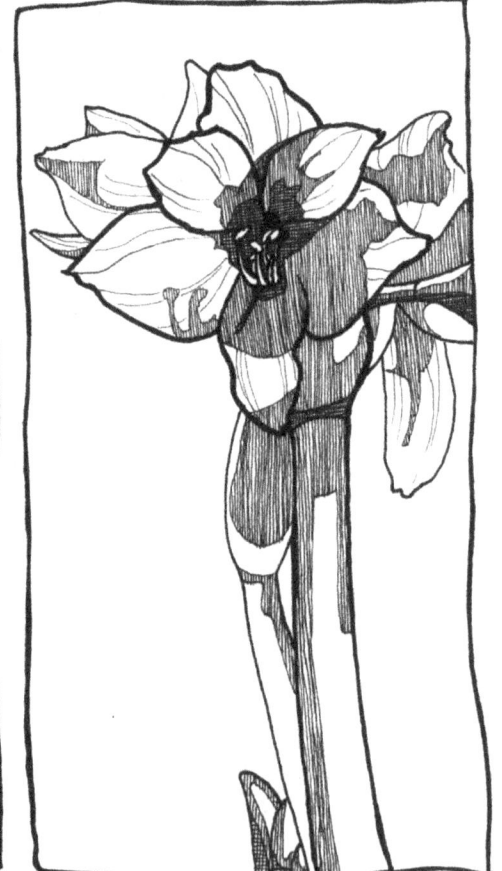

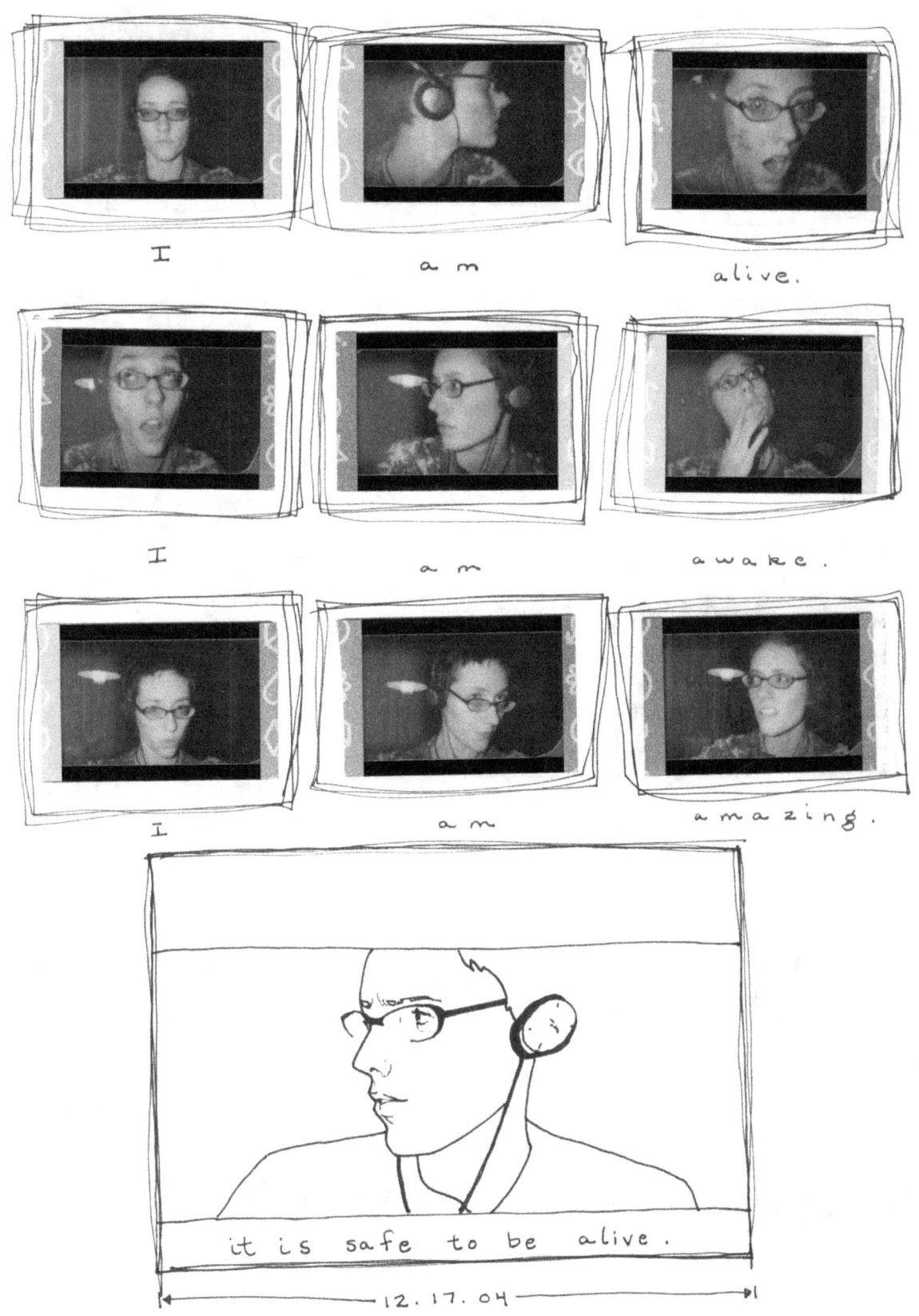

I   a m   alive.

I   a m   awake.

I   a m   amazing.

it is safe to be alive.

12.17.04

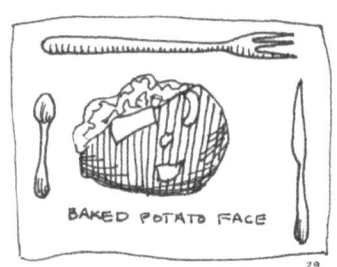

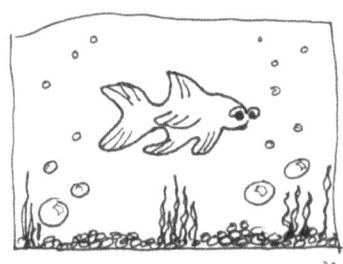

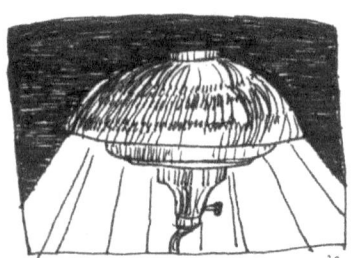

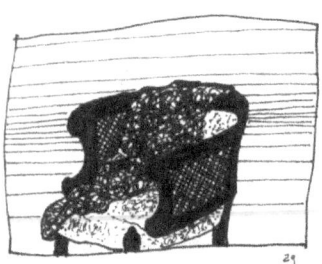

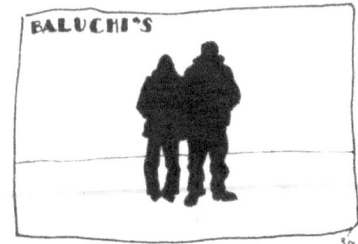

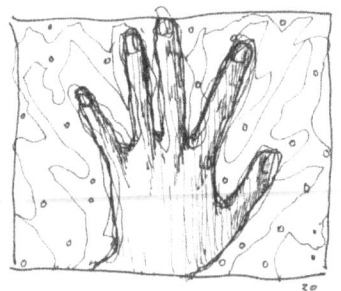

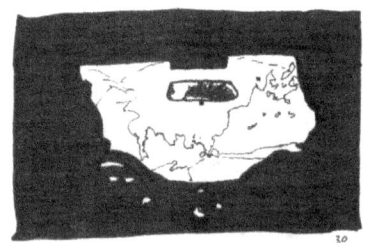

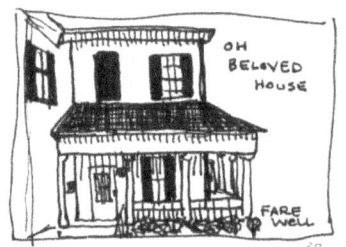

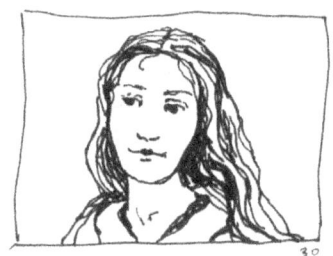

all is quiet ...

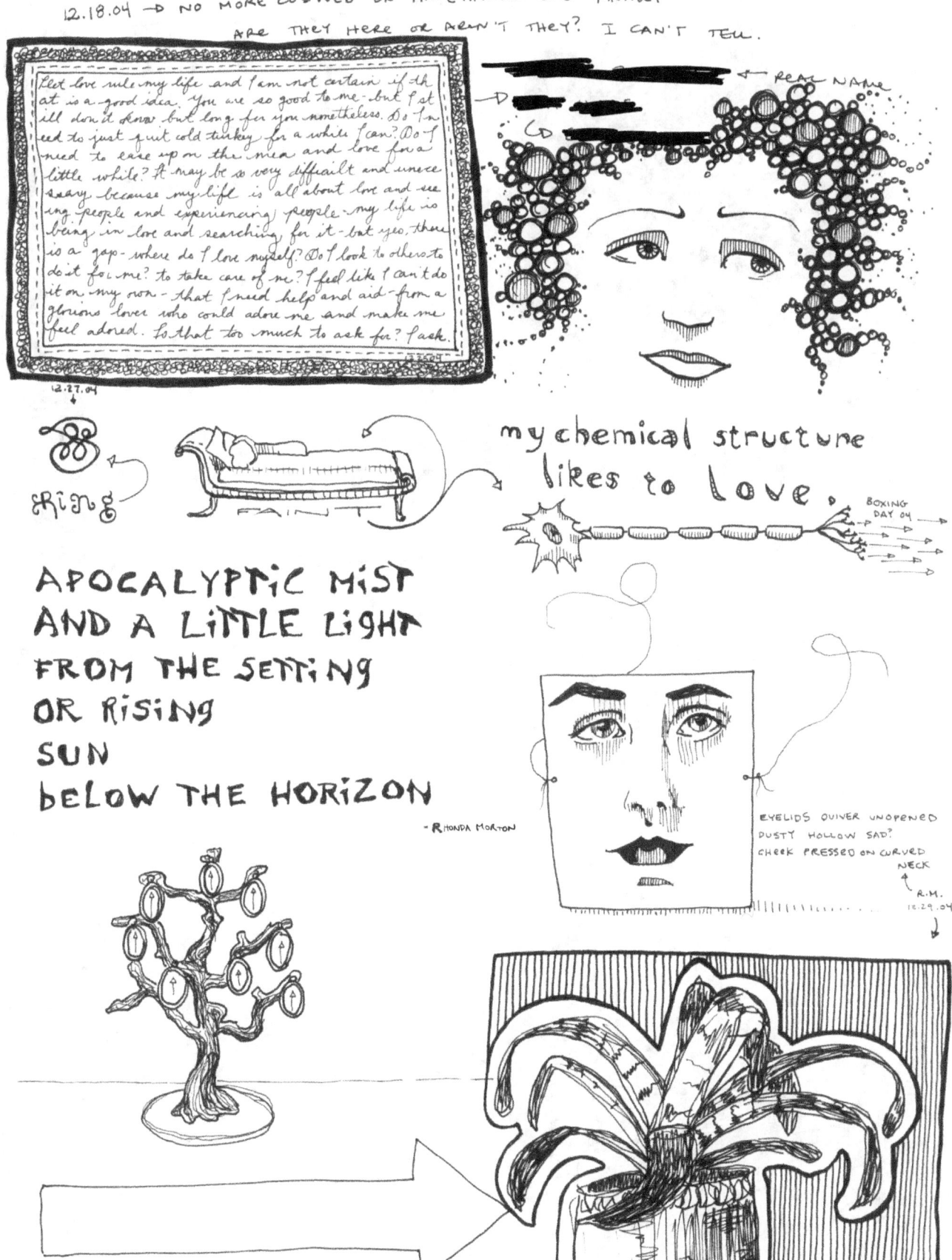

12.18.04 → NO MORE COBWEB ON THE CHANDELIERS - FINALLY

ARE THEY HERE OR AREN'T THEY? I CAN'T TELL.

← REAL NAME

Let love rule my life and I am not certain if that is a good idea. You are so good to me - but I still don't know but long for you nonetheless. Do I need to just quit cold turkey for a while I can? Do I need to ease up on the mea and love for a little while? It may be so very difficult and unnecessary, because my life is all about love and seeing people and experiencing people - my life is being in love and searching for it - but yes, there is a gap - where do I love myself? Do I look to others to do it for me? to take care of me? I feel like I can't do it on my own - that I need help and aid - from a glorious lover who could adore me and make me feel adored. Is that too much to ask for? I ask.

12.27.04

Rising

FAINT

my chemical structure
likes to love.

BOXING DAY 04

APOCALYPTIC MIST
AND A LITTLE LIGHT
FROM THE SETTING
OR RISING
SUN
BELOW THE HORIZON

- Rhonda Morton

EYELIDS QUIVER UNOPENED
DUSTY HOLLOW SAD?
CHEEK PRESSED ON CURVED
NECK

R.M.
12.29.04

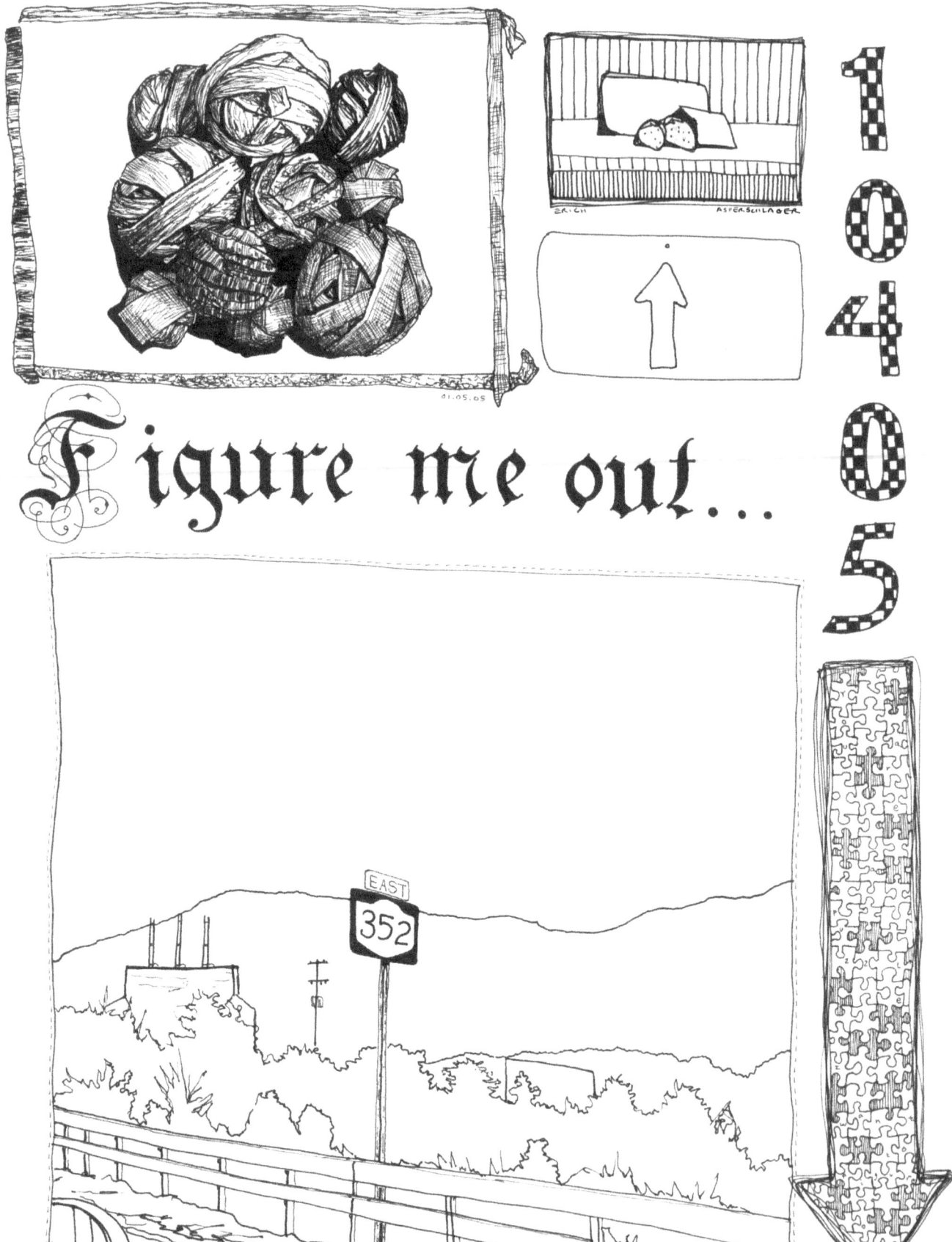

Figure me out...

01.05.05

1
0
4
0
5

01.05.05

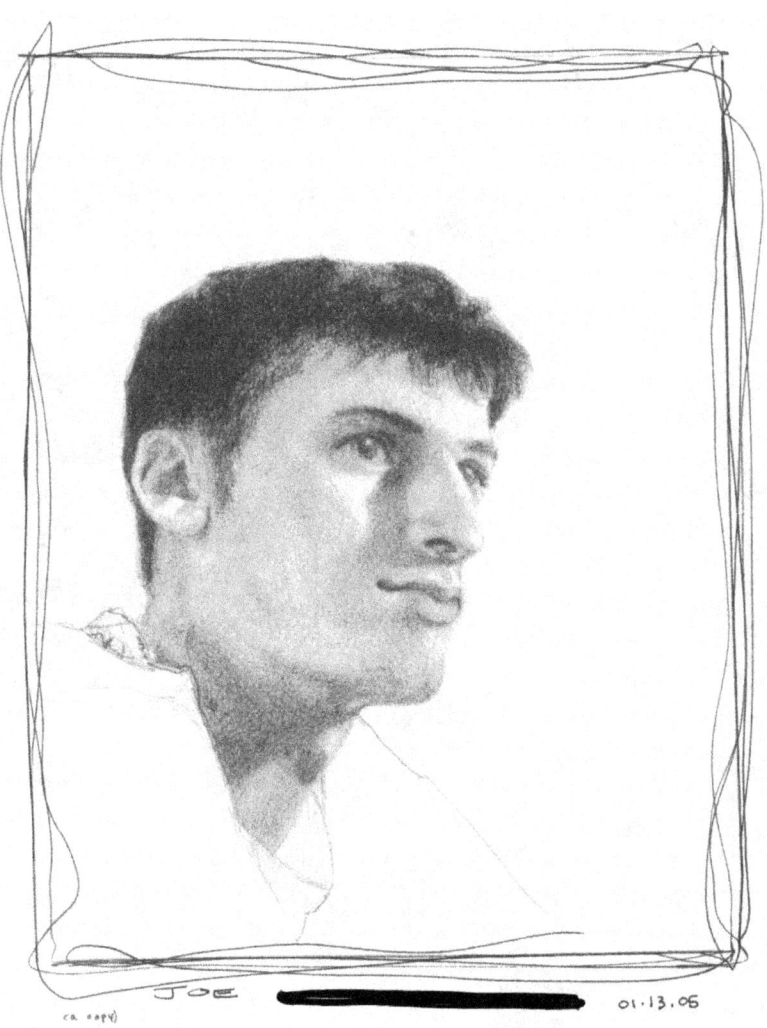

JOE ████████████████ 01·13·05

(a copy)

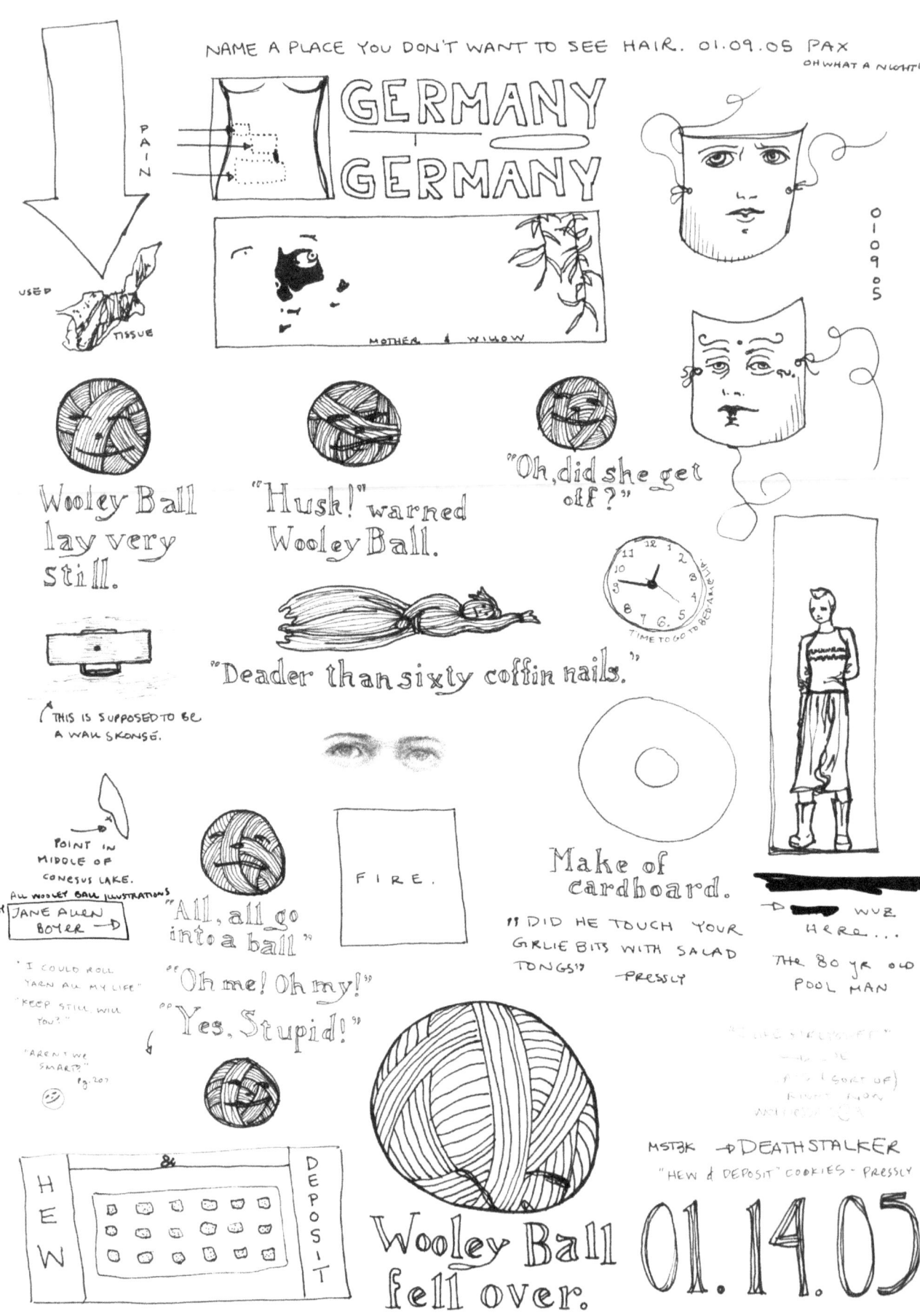

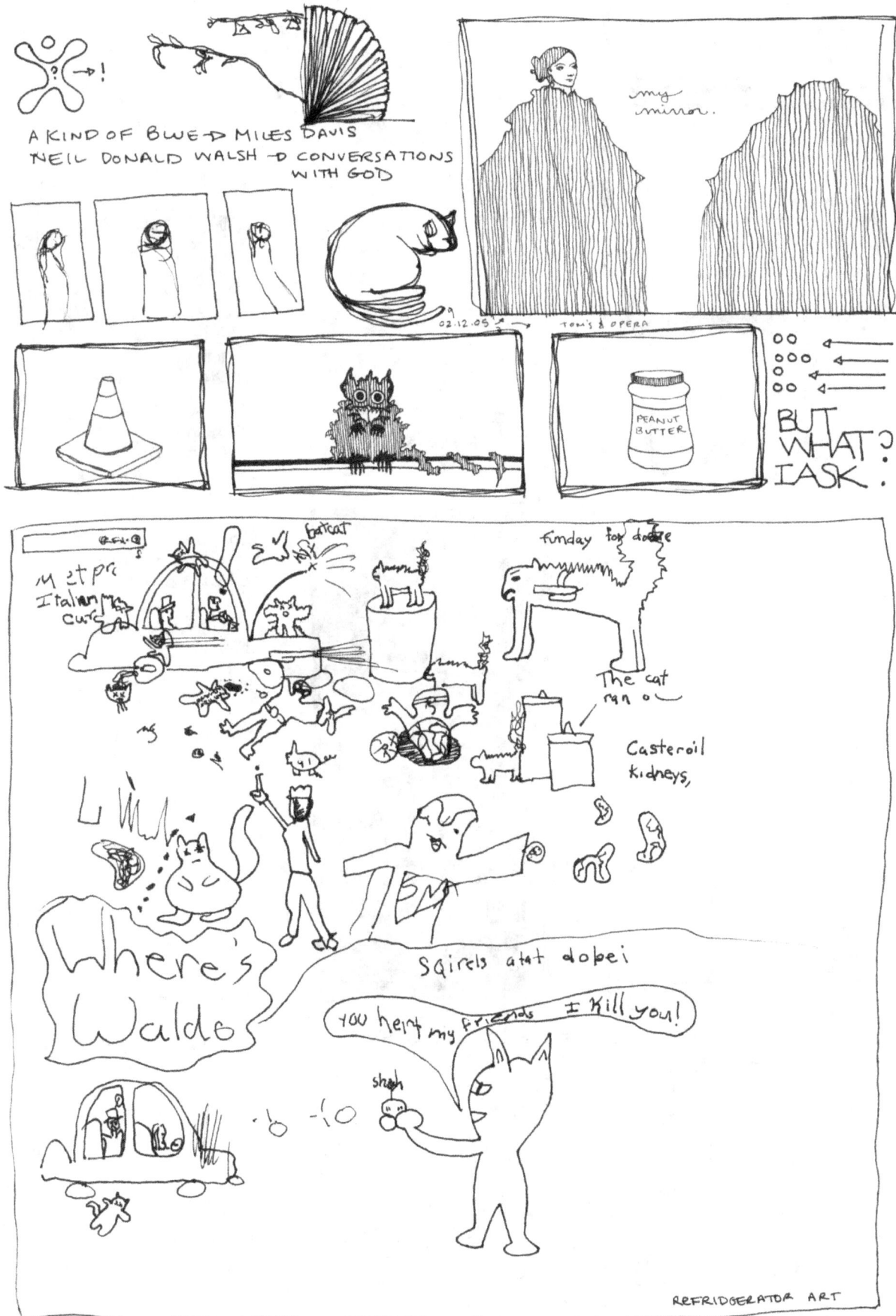

French: Question: Quelle différence y a-t-il entre un chewing-gum et un avion?
Réponse: Le chewing-gum colle et l'avion décolle!

4

French: Question: Je porte des lunettes mais je ne vois pas. Qui suis-je?
Réponse: Un nez!

3

French: Question: Pourquoi faut-il fermer un oeil quand on vise?
Réponse: Parce que si on ferme les deux, -on ne voit plus rien!

11

FROM ENGLISH CHRISTMAS CRACKERS

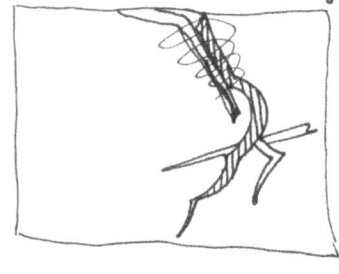

down to.

AMELIA, WHAT ARE YOU DOING WITH YOUR LIFE ??!
011905

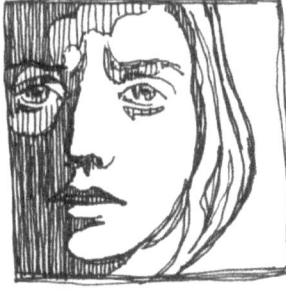

01 2405

G F R

σ μ n s x̄

I DON'T LIKE GREG A. HE'S MEAN AND HAS COOTIES. 012905
SOMEDAY I'M GOING TO PLUMMET HIM HEAD FIRST INTO A LARGE SNOW BANK.

it's funny how the human mind works, with all of its twists and turns. so, don't let me down. i want to keep you around 2nd verse

do you want me to paint you? in indian yellow and ultramarine blue. the light would be so soft. in those shadows, i could get lost...

ah ah ah ah ah ah ah ah ah ah ah ah ah ah ah ah ah ah ah ah
012605

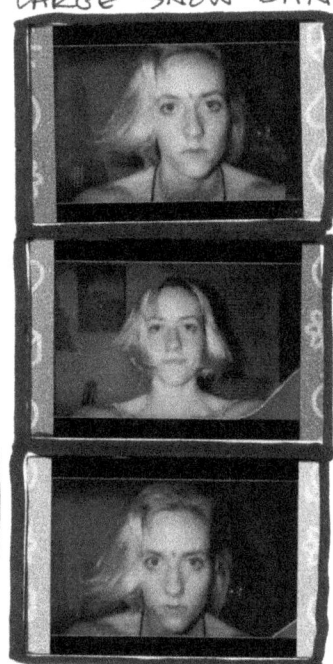

NO SWING

YET.

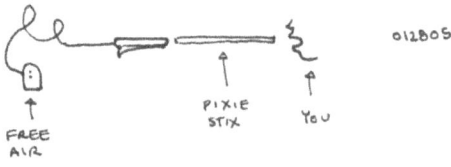

FREE AIR
PIXIE STIX
YOU

012805

I VOLTAIRED MY PANTS THIS MORNING — DAN
→ MEXICAN RESTAURANT PLAYS "WEATHER WITH YOU" 012905

(AM I IN MIDDLE SCHOOL AGAIN?)

01.31.05

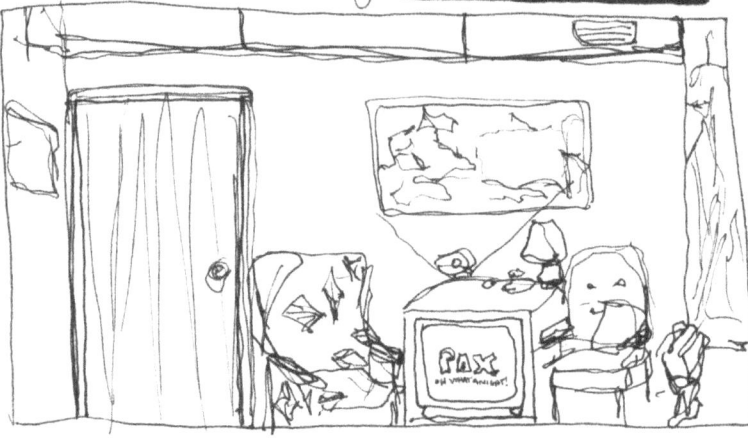

PAX

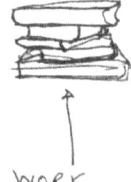

LADY BUG THAT JUST VISITED ME →

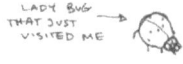

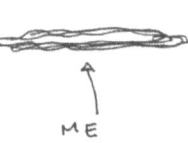

WORK

ME

OH, THIS AGAIN IS IT? SHOULD BE FUN ONCE AGAIN, YES? OH, QUITE SO I THINK I SHOULD NEGLECT SPACING AND PUNCTUATION. I FORGOT RIGHT THEN HA WELL MAYBE PUNCTUATION IS GOOD TO KEEP. AH, YES. WHEN PEOPLE LAUGH AT CENTURIES OLD OPERA, I CAN'T HELP BUT LAUGH TOO. OH MOZART, YOU FIEND! IT'S SO DANGEROUS TO WRITE IN HERE LIKE I DO - SO DANGEROUS. THE ONLY WAY THAT THIS WRITING COULD EVER BE SEEN SIGNIFICANT IS IF I BECOME FAMOUS (EVEN THEN, IT'D HAVE TO BE OF THE DEAD FAME VARIETY) AND I DON'T SEE THAT HAPPENING. EITHER THAT, OR I FIND SOME TRULY AMAZING MAN WHO IS MY TRUE LOVE AND HE WANTS TO KNOW ME AS BEST AS POSSIBLE INSIDE AND OUT, AND THAT COULD BE YEARS FROM NOW. WHAT IS WRONG WITH MY PEN?! SUCH SLOSHING AROUND IN YOUR OPERA MOZART - YOU NUT, AND WITH THE UTMOST SECRECY I ASK I ASK I ASK, AM I A JOKER? AM I SUCH TO THAT I AM SUCH? I AM SITTING HERE WAITING EVER SO PATIENTLY AND SO PATIENTLY I SAY SO PATIENTLY SO PATIENTLY IN THE FRONT SEE YOU SOON WAITING PATIENTLY EVER SO PATIENTLY AND MAYBE YOU THINK THAT I'M ANNOYING AND BOTHERSOME WHICH IS WHY YOU'RE GOING TO STAND ME UP I SAY - STAND ME UP I SAY STAND ME UP PATIENTLY I SAY SO PATIENTLY I WAIT SO PATIENTLY GET OVER HERE. DON'T STAY AWAY TOO LONG - DASHED AND DRAWN YOUR PARADOX AND MY FIREWORKS CARRY THIS KEY AROUND WITH YOU TO REMIND YOURSELF OF ME YOU KNOW THE WIND BUT YOU ONLY GET IS YOUR HANDS SO YOU BETTER SPREAD THEM WIND CARRY THIS RING AROUND WITH YOU TO REMIND YOURSELF OF ME THIS IS A TRAIN MANIC CLATTERING BATTERS AT ME AS I COUPLE THE LIFE I'VE KNOWN TO THE LIFE YET TO BE TRACKS VISIBLE BELOW RUN STRAIGHT WHILE I'M SLAMMED SIDE TO SIDE ON THIS RICKETY BRIDGE JOLTED AND JARRED IN THIS NOISY ENVELOPE OF TIME IMMORTALLY SUITED MOMENTS THE DEMISE OF SEEMS WITHIN THESE VERY WORDS YOU CAN HEAR MY HEART STUMBLING. CARRY THIS KEY AROUND WITH YOU TO REMIND YOURSELF OF ME YOUR PARADOX MY FIREWORKS YOUR PARADOX MY FIREWORKS YOUR PARADOX MY FIREWORKS YOUR PARADOX MY FIREWORKS. WHAT AM I DOING WHAT IS GOING ON? A BLACKBIRD TRAPPED IN THE WALLS OF THIS WHITE HOUSE I THINK ITS WING IS BROKEN I WISH I COULD PULL IT OUT YOU'VE BEEN IN HERE FOR DAYS SITTING ON THE GREEN COUCH WATCHING THE CLOCK CALCULATING NUMBERS I WISH I COULD TELL YOU TAKE A RISK FAIL OR FLY IF YOU FALL YOU MIGHT DIE BUT AT LEAST YOU WILL KNOW WHAT IT FEELS LIKE ARE YOU BLUEBEARD WITH THE LOCKED ROOM HANDING ME THE KEYS AND TELLING ME NOT TO GO IN I KNOW I MUST SEE WHAT'S INSIDE TAKE A RISK FLY OR FALL IF YOU FAIL ONCE AT ALL THEN AT LEAST YOU WILL KNOW THAT ITS POSSIBLE OH MY OH ME I HAVE SENT YOU A LETTER ON THE 24 OF 2 OF 2005 I HAVE SENT YOU A LETTER AND I HOPE IT DOESN'T AFFECT MY STANDING MY LIFE IN A BAD WAY OH THE WAY I IMAGINE IT ALL TO WORK OUT. OH SO LOVELY - MY FANTASY REINCARNATE I WILL ALWAYS BE IN LOVE WITH YOU. WILL IT ALL WORKOUT? I'M SO IN LOVE WITH YOU - ALWAYS HAVE ALWAYS WILL BE. MATISSE'S FISH & OXANNA NEWPALTZ. YOU. YOU. YOU. I AWAIT A LETTER FROM YOU. I LOOK FOR YOU EVERYWHERE I GO. I THINK I HAD A DREAM ABOUT YOU LAST NIGHT. I THINK I DREAMT OF YOU AND SOMETHING IMPORTANT HAPPENED BUT WHAT WAS IT? I'M SO SLEEPY. I WISH I COULD FALL ASLEEP IN YOUR ARMS. I MISS YOU. I WANT TO CALL YOU. VISIT YOU. SEE YOUR LOVELY FACE AGAIN. HEAR YOUR VOICE AND SEE THE WAY YOU MOVE. SMELL YOU AGAIN. OH I MISS YOU. IF WE GOT MARRIED SO MANY PEOPLE WOULD BE SO UPSET WITH ME. I HAVE GOLD FINGERTIPS. AM I DOING THE RIGHT THING? LOOKING FOR YOU AGAIN. AM I GETTING MYSELF INTO TROUBLE? SHOULD I WRITE YOUR MOTHER AND SEEK HER ADVICE? SHOULD I CALL YOU TONIGHT? SHOULD I BE PATIENT AND WAIT A FEW YEARS TO SEE IF YOU'VE WRITT

OH OH LOVE. MY LOVE. I MISS YOU SO MUCH. I WON WHEN I LEFT. I WONDER WHAT THE HOUSE LOOKS AM TRYING MY BEST TO BE GOOD ABOUT THE C THAT SONG THAT PLAYED ON THE ALARM CLOCK PERTINENT TO SO RIGHT. OH I MISS YOU SO MUCH SUNSHINE SO BADLY ALL THE TIME. I WONDER CLOSE BY. IF YOU SEE ME DURING THE DAY AND IF YOU STILL LOVE ME. I WONDER IF YOU'LL GO TO THE PROBABLY NOT. I FEEL LIKE LOOKING FOR YOU IN UCH. I'M GOING TO FALL ASLEEP. I'M SO SLEEPY AN ANNOYING SOUND EFFECT. I WANT TO FALL THEN AGAIN, IF I GO HOME, I COULD SLEEP, DO S ERS, WRITE SOME EMAIL, AND TAKE ANOTHER N THINK I MIGHT JUST GO HOME THEN. I COULD OK. TIME TO GO HOME NOW. I LOVE YOU. I LOVE WALKING TO CLASS AND I RAN TO FO WOW YOU AND ME EMAIL YOU AND I JUST DON'T KNOW IF YOU WILL YOU. SO WHEN I SIT IN CLASS AND WANT TO SMASH A WHEN I START CRYING ITS GONE TOO FAR. FEBRUAR YOU'VE READ MY EMAIL AND HOW YOU REACTED. IF ME. IF YOU LOVE ME. IF YOU'RE WAITING FOR SOME- ELSE. IF YOU'D BE WITH ME AGAIN. IF YOUR MOTHER ED. SO SOMEDAY WE WILL TALK AGAIN. BUT I HAVE WHILE. THAT YOU'RE TESTING ME. BUT MAYBE INDEED MUCH AND CAN'T FORGIVE ME. I'M GOING TO THE RIVE IF YOU'D MAGICALLY BE THERE. OH, ME AND MY FANT SILLY AMÉLIE. AH, BUT YOU ARE MY NINO - PLEASE COM OW THAT I'VE ALWAYS THOUGHT THAT WE WOULD BE T MANY HARD TIMES. AND I THINK THAT THIS PAST T ANY BRIDGES AND WE'D HAVE A LOT OF FORGIVING T HAVE TO TEST MY PATIENCE AND DETERMINATION. BUT I IS HAND THAT I SHOULD JUST LET YOU GO BECAUSE YOU'RE HATE ME NOW. YOU PROBABLY DON'T WANT ME ANY MORE

EN A LETTER? AND THEN WRITE ANOTHER DER IF YOU REALLY DO LIKE ME LIKE YOU SAID LIKE. IF YOU'VE CHANGED ANYTHING. I LAS S THING. THEY'RE PLAYING U2 AGAIN AND WOKE ME UP THIS MORNING WAS SO RIGHT NOW. I WANT TO WATCH ETERNAL IF YOU THINK ABOUT ME AT ALL. IF YOU'RE IT MEANS ANYTHING TO YOU. I WONDER IF MOVIE THING TONIGHT AND IF WE'D TALK THE LIBRARY SOMEWHERE. I MISS YOU SOM I AM SO SLEEPY. WHEN DOVES CRY. THAT'S ASLEEP. BUT I SHOULD GO TO THIS PD EVENT CHOLARSHIP THING, CALL MOM, EAT LEFT OV P AND WOULDN'T HAVE TO DIG OUT MY CAR. I SING A LITTLE BIT. SO MUCH U2 NEW ALBUM YOU. I LOVE YOU. I LOVE YOU. I LOVE YOU... I FEEL LIKE A STALKER BECAUSE I SAW YOU TODAY JUST WATCH AS YOU WALKED AWAY. BUT THAT MADE TALK TO ME. I WANT TO TALK TO ME. I LOVE LL OF MY FINGERS WITH A BASEBALL BAT. OUCH I WONDER WHAT YOU'RE DOING RIGHT NOW IF YOU'RE GOING TO WRITE ME BACK IF YOU HATE THING. IF YOU'RE IN LOVE WITH SOMEONE STILL LIKES ME. IF SHE THINKS I'M BEING MISGUID A FEELING THAT I'M GOING TO BE SINGLE FOR A YOU NO LONGER LOVE ME BECAUSE YOU HATE ME SO RT TONIGHT. TO THINK. TO FREEZE. AND I WONDE ASIES. WILL I EVER GET OVER THESE FANTASIES? E THROUGH FOR ME. PLEASE BE MY NINO. I KN OGETHER BUT ONLY AFTER WE WENT THROUGH HING WAS THE HARDEST. THOUGH I BURNED M ING AND RIGHT NOW I DON'T KNOW IF YOU'RE READY TO FORGIVE ME. I GUESS I STILL

HAVE TO TEST MY PATIENCE AND DETERMINATION. BUT I'M NOT GOING TO LIE AND SAY THAT NO VOICES TELL ME I'M BEING LONELY AND FOOL IS HAND THAT I SHOULD JUST LET YOU GO BECAUSE YOU'RE NOT RIGHT FOR ME I STILL HAVEN'T HEARD FROM YOU. I KNOW YOU MUST REALLY HATE ME NOW. YOU PROBABLY DON'T WANT ME ANY MORE. I MUST WRITE YOU THAT LETTER OF APOLOGY, AND IT HAS TO BE GOOD. I KNOW BECAUSE THIS IS SO IMPORTANT TO GET YOU BACK. IT'S SO IMPORTANT TO ME THAT YOU LOVE ME AGAIN AND BE WITH ME AGAIN. OH. I AM JUST LIKE A CRAZY HEROINE IN SOME VICTORIAN NO - MORE LIKE A 1920'S F. SCOTT FITZGERALD HEROINE WHO LOVES TOO MANY AND KEEPS TOO FEW LAUNDROMATS ARE STRANGE PLACES WITH LOTS OF STRANGE NOISES AND STRANGE PEOPLE. I WONDER IF I'LL EVER SEE YOU AGAIN. I KNOW I WILL. I WILL SEE YOU AGAIN SOMEDAY, BUT WILL I KISS YOU AGAIN? WHY DOES A VOICE SAY NO? SUCH TORTURE! I MISS YOU SO MUCH. I WISH. I WISH THIS COULD ALL HAPPEN ALL OVER. TRY THIS AGAIN. TRY THIS ONE MORE TIME. SAVE #7 FOR YOU. BUT YOUR PRIDE. YOUR HURT YOUR STUBBORNNESS, YOU PROBABLY WANT TO TEST THIS CHANGE OF HEART AND I DON'T BLAME YOU. I'D DO THE SAME IF I WERE IN YOUR SHOES. I'D WANT TO MAKE SURE BEFORE I TOOK A SECOND RISK. OH. AMELIA. WHAT ARE YOU DOING? OH I DON'T KNOW. I'M TRYING TO FIGURE IT OUT AS I GO ALONG. I DO KNOW THAT IF YOU WERE TO TAKE ME BACK TODAY, I'D BE SO OVERWHELMINGLY HA PPY AND OVERJOYED. I'D WEEP TEARS OF JOY. I'D BE DANCING IN MY HEART. DOES YOUR PROPOSAL STILL STAND? WOULD YOU EVER TALK TO ME AGAIN, LET ALONE MARRY ME? I HOPE YOU DO TALK TO ME AGAIN, MY HEART WOULD POUND RESTLESSLY IF I EVER GOT A LETTER FROM YOU AGAIN. I WANT TO BE WITH YOU AGAIN. PLEASE LET ME BACK INTO YOUR LIFE. I NEED TO MEDITATE MORE AGAIN. I THINK THAT WOULD BE SO HELPFUL IN ALL AREAS OF MY LIFE. IT WOULD HELP ME BE HAPPY AGAIN, I KNOW IT. OH AMELIA. OH RYAN. IT'S NOTHING MALICIOUS. PLEASE TRUST ME ON THAT. IT'S NOTHING MALICIOUS. ONLY ME LOVING YOU WITH ALL MY HEART AND KNOWING IT AGAIN. BUT RYAN YOU ARE SO DISTRUSTFUL. YOU SHUT DOWN AND SHUT OUT SO MUCH FROM YOUR LIFE. DON'T MISS THIS CHANCE. PLEASE COME BACK TO MY LOVE AND STAY WITH ME THIS TIME. LET'S DO IT AT THE SAME TIME, THIS TIME. LET'S FALL IN LOVE, AGAIN. 03

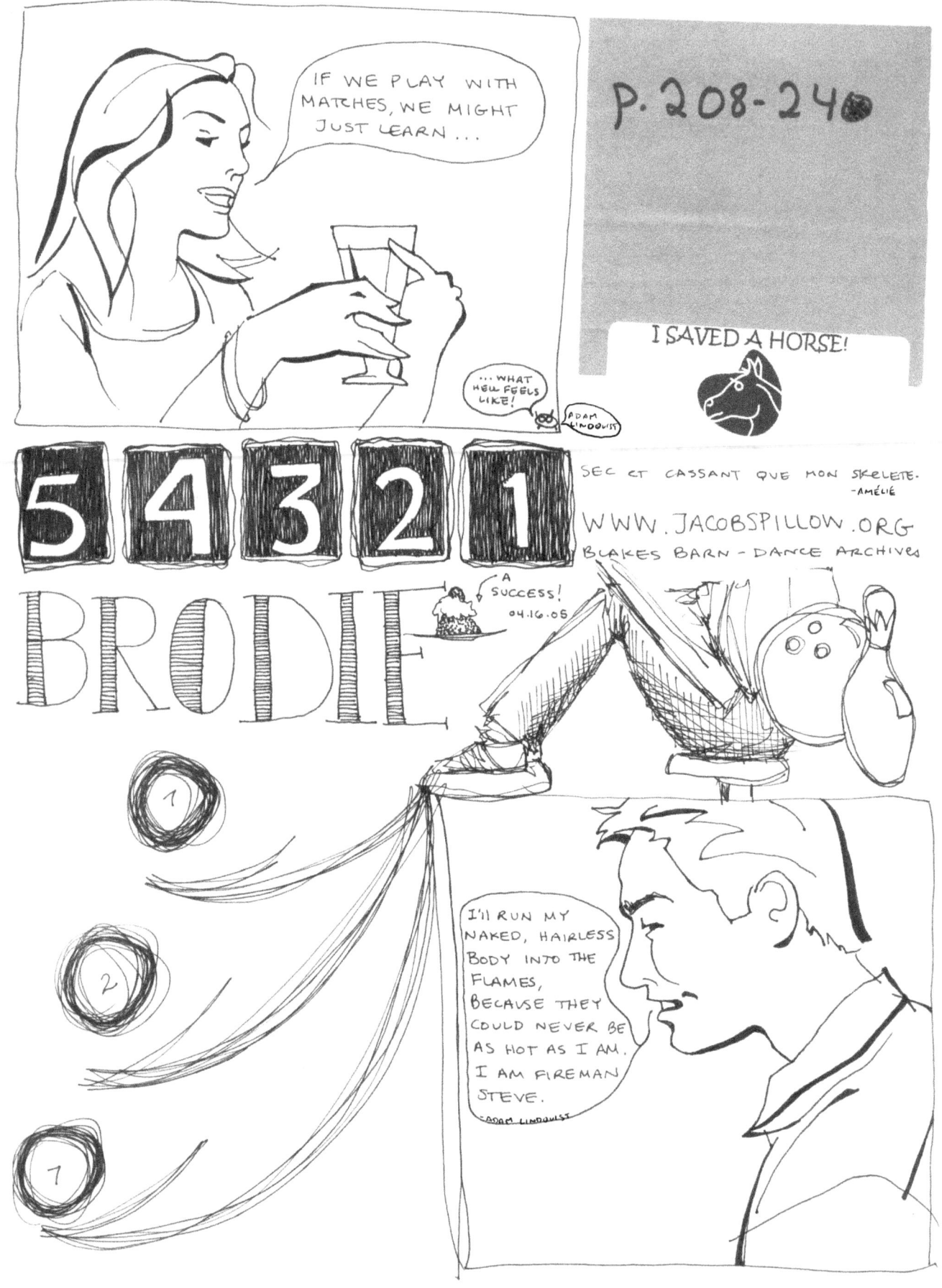

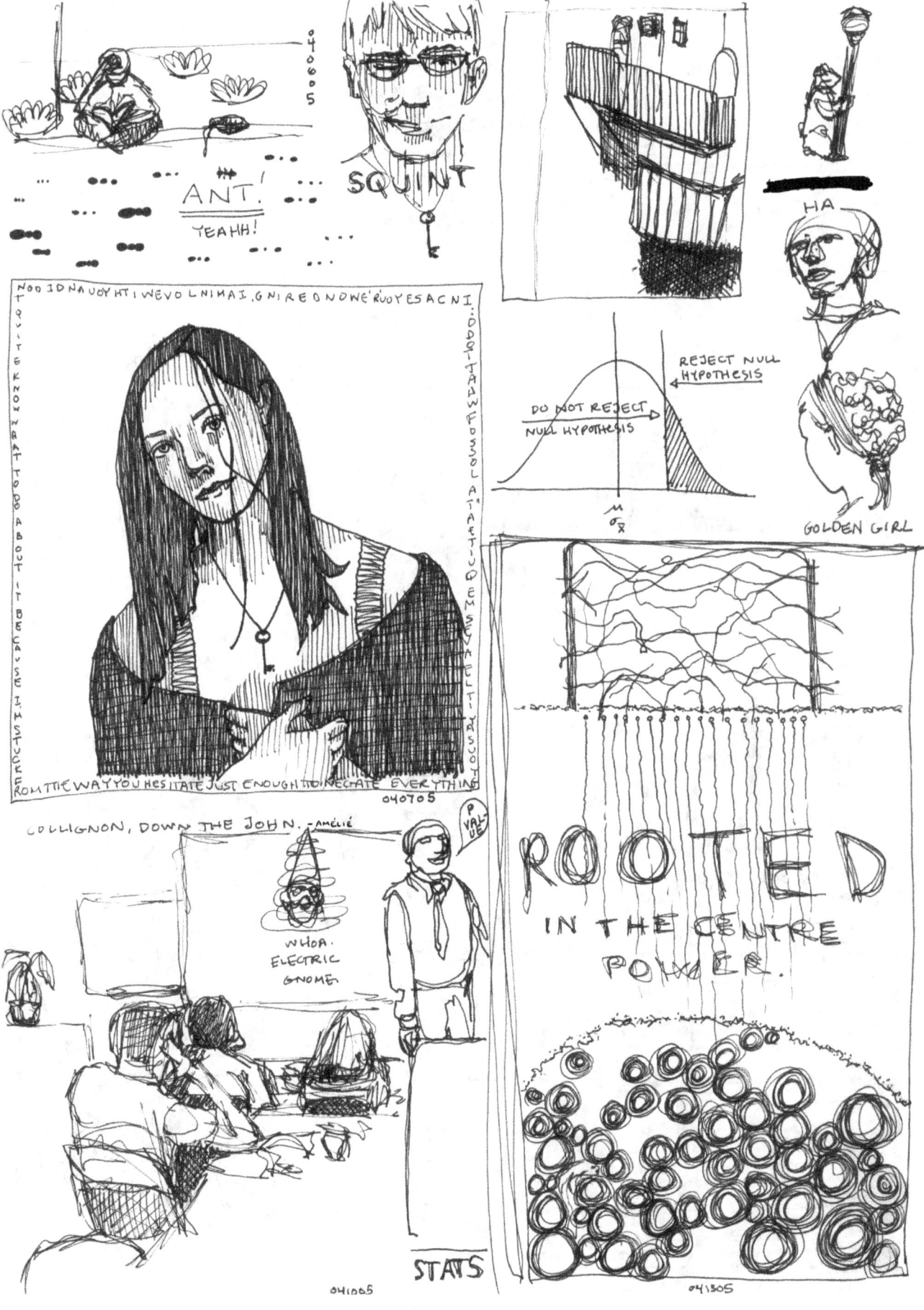

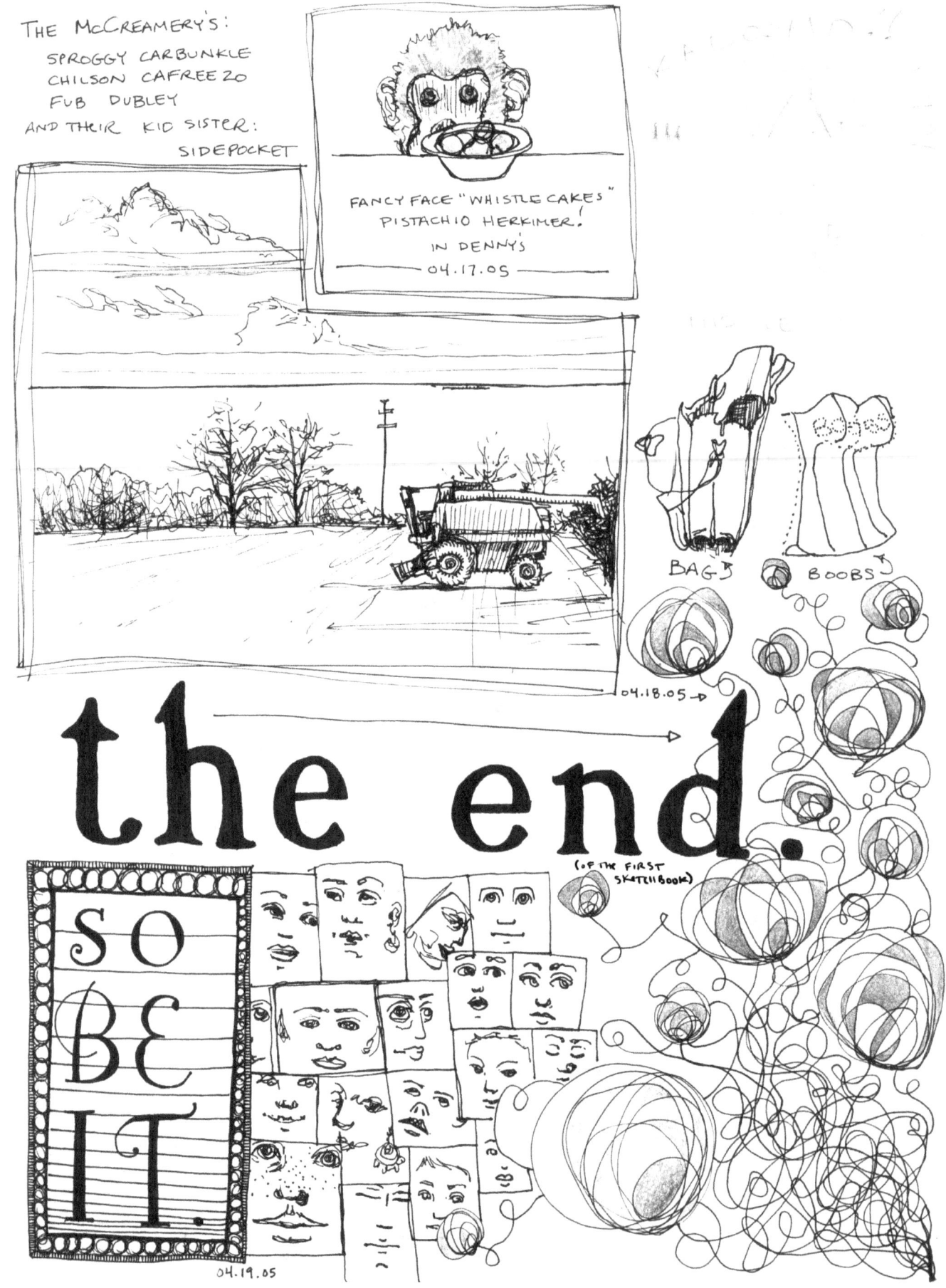

THE McCREAMERY'S:
SPROGGY CARBUNKLE
CHILSON CAFREEZO
FUB DUBLEY
AND THEIR KID SISTER:
SIDEPOCKET

FANCY FACE "WHISTLE CAKES"
PISTACHIO HERKIMER!
IN DENNY'S
— 04.17.05 —

BAG

BOOBS

04.18.05 →

the end.
(OF THE FIRST SKETCHBOOK)

SO BE IT.

04.19.05

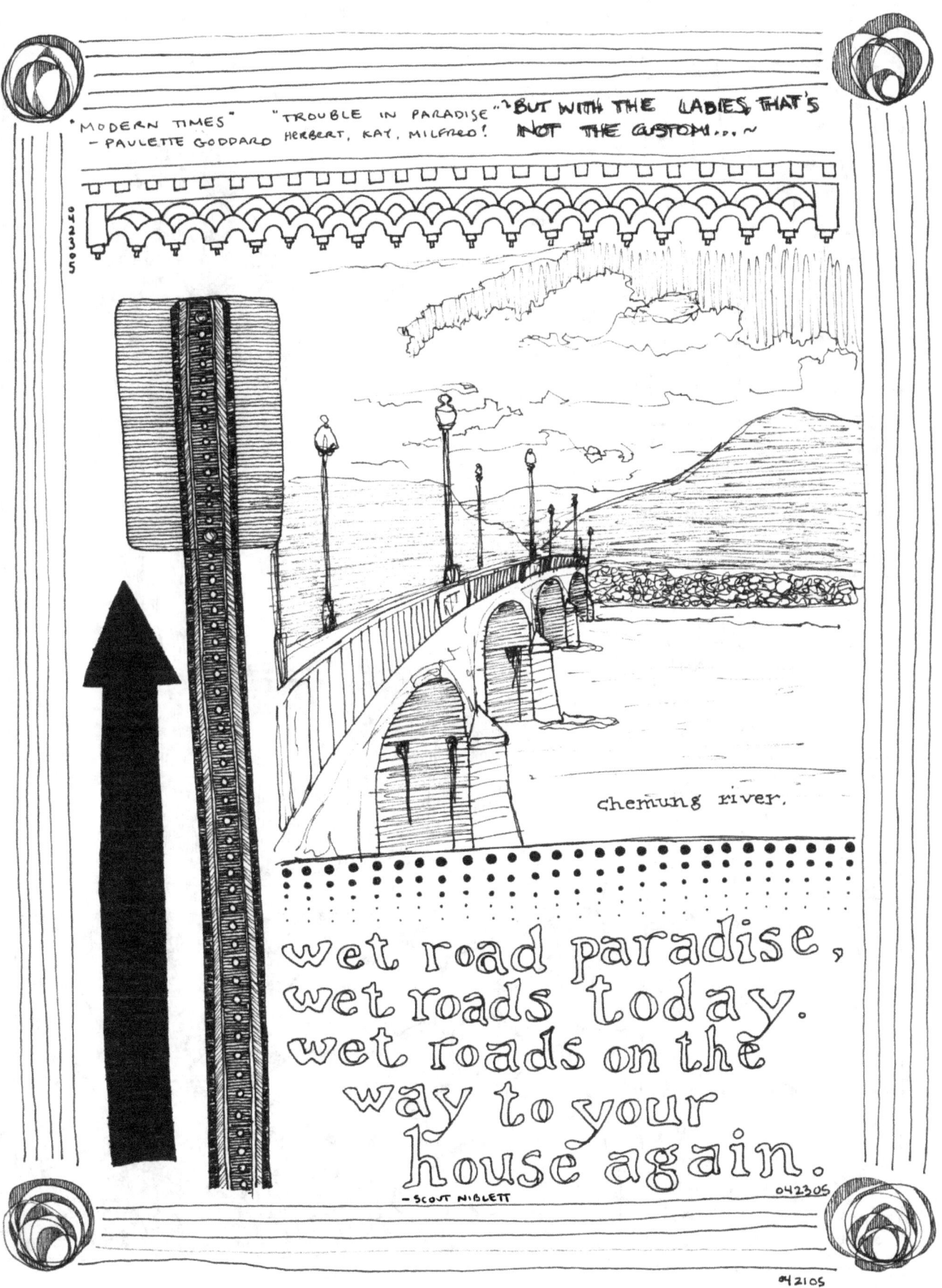

"MODERN TIMES"   "TROUBLE IN PARADISE" "BUT WITH THE LADIES THAT'S
 -PAULETTE GODDARD HERBERT, KAY, MILFRED!   NOT THE CUSTOM...~

chemung river.

wet road paradise,
wet roads today.
wet roads on the
way to your
house again.
 -SCOUT NIBLETT   042305

042105

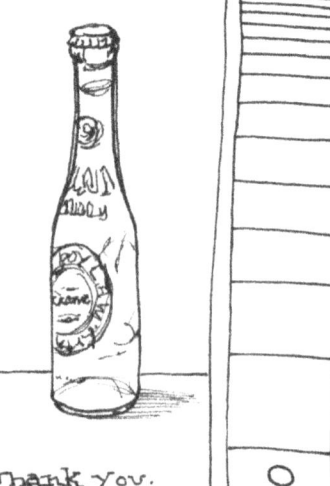

Thank you.

0

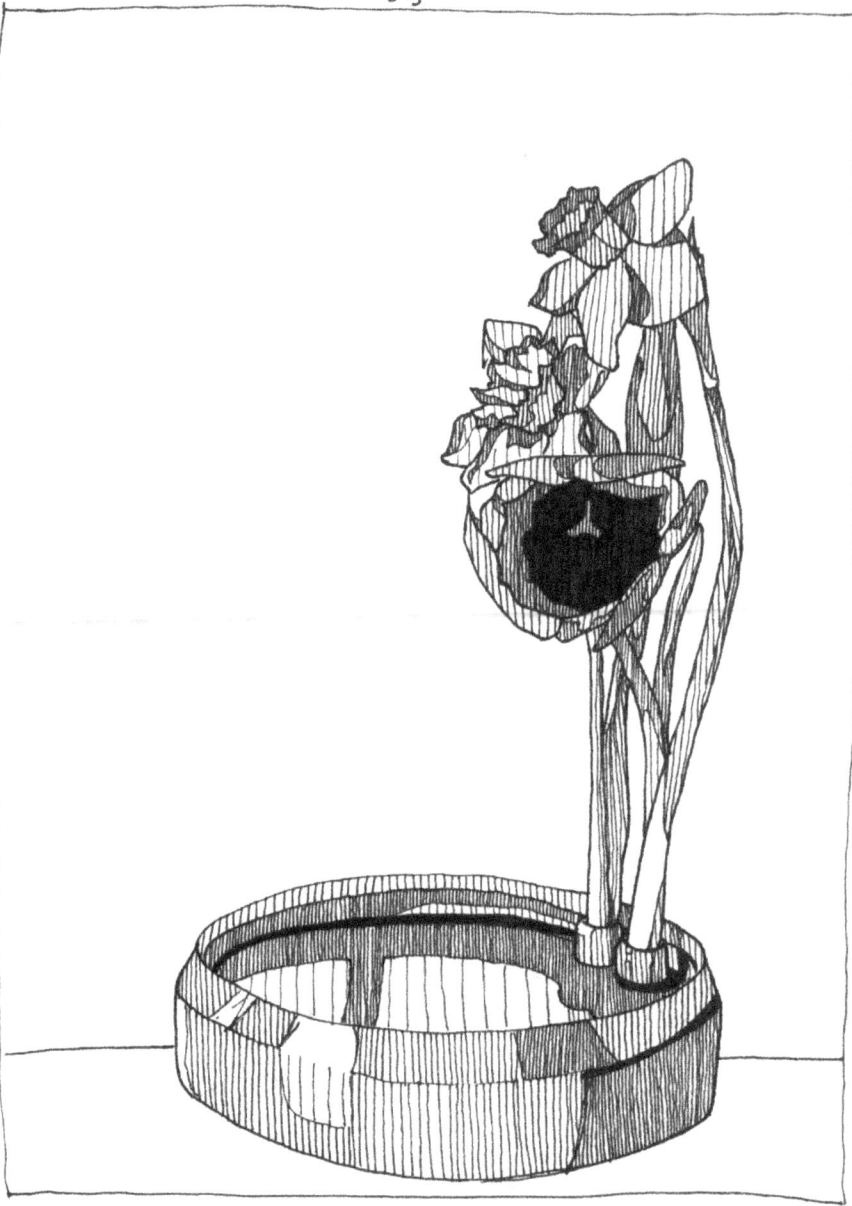

"STOP." I IMPLORED,
"DON'T GO. YOU CAN
DANCE OF COURSE, AS
MUCH AS YOU PLEASE,
BUT DON'T
STAY AWAY
TOO LONG.
COME BACK AGAIN,
COME BACK AGAIN."

SHE LAUGHED AS SHE
GOT UP. I IMAGIN-
ED HER TO BE TALLER,
SHE WAS SLENDER, BUT
NOT TALL. AGAIN I
WAS REMINDED OF
SOME ONE. OF WHOM
? I COULD NOT MAKE
OUT.

"YOU'RE COMING
BACK?"

"I'M COMING
BACK, BUT IT MAY
BE HALF AN HOUR OR
AN HOUR, PERHAPS....
SHUT YOUR EYES AND
SLEEP FOR A LITTLE."

STEPPENWOLF PG·103 042605

042605

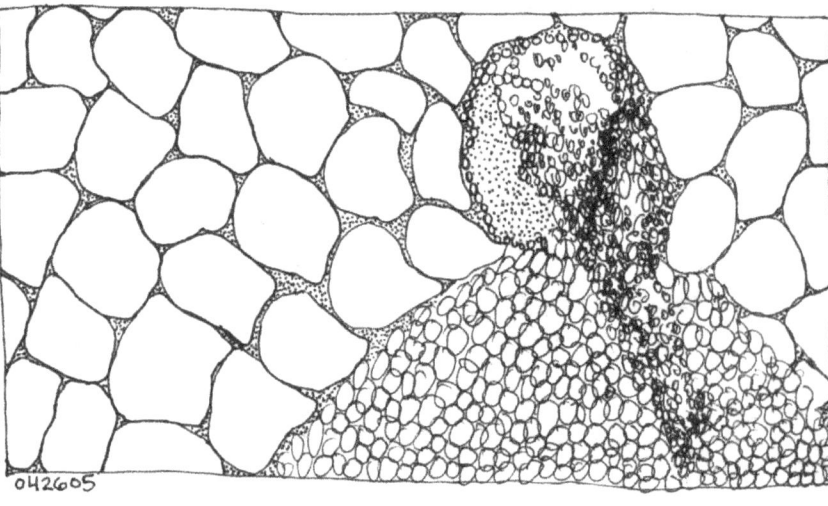

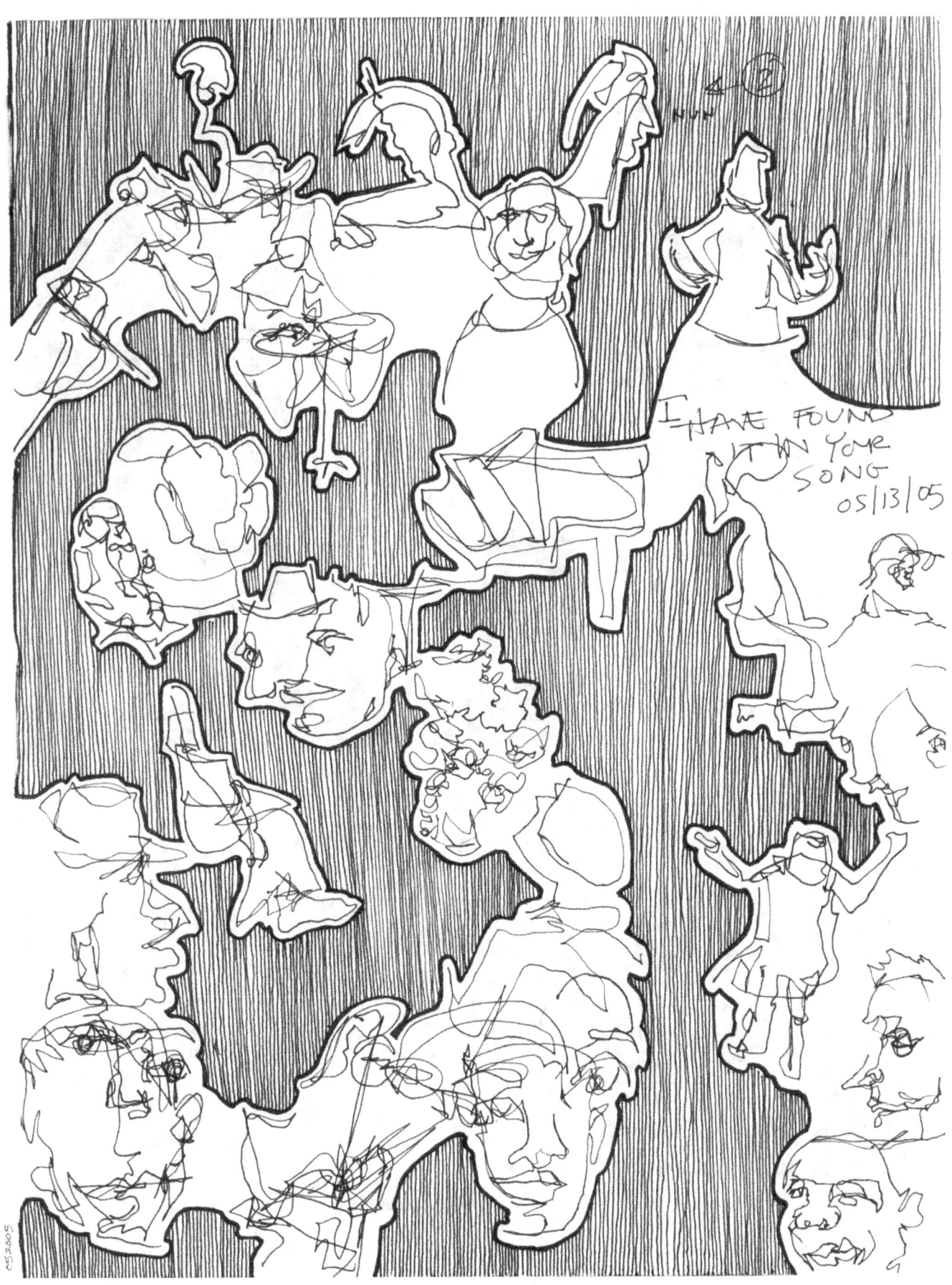

I HAVE FOUND
IT IN YOUR
SONG
05/13/05

labori
us wal
ks/ma
intena
nce an
d pen
tinen
ce/pa
ying b
ills an

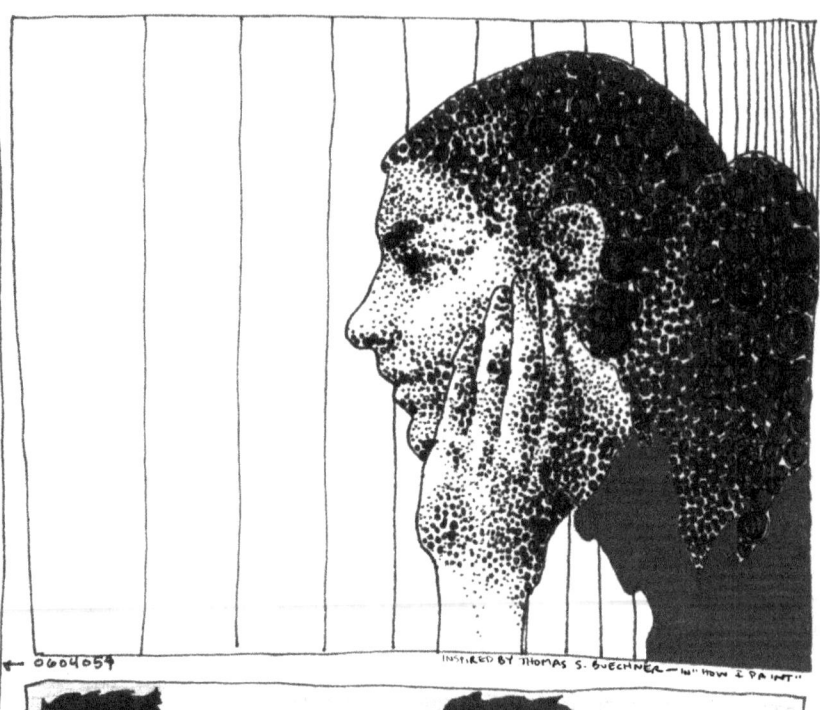

← 0604054

INSPIRED BY THOMAS S. BUECHNER — IN "HOW I PAINT"

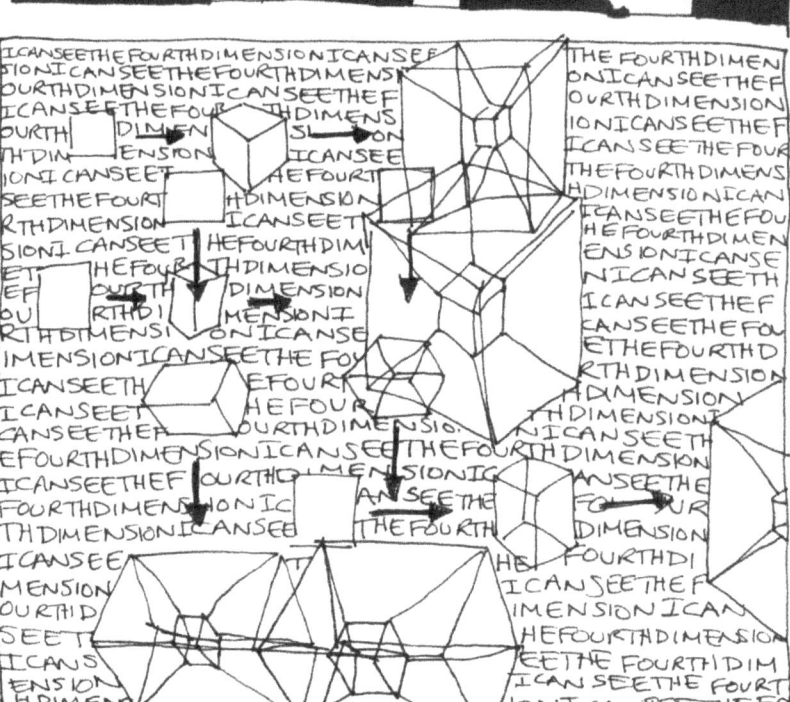

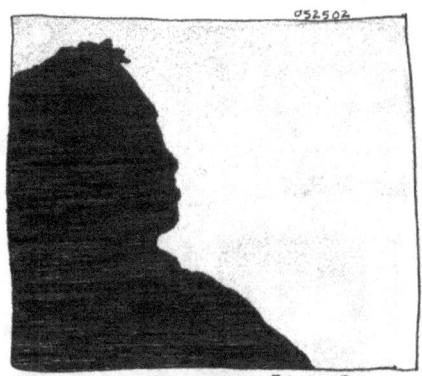

he explained to me the stars.

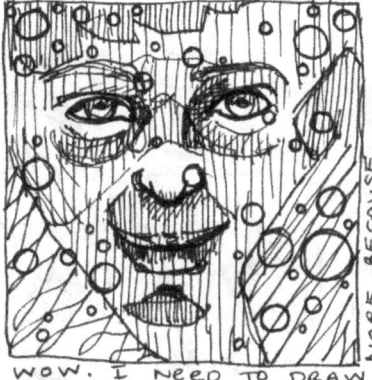

WOW. I NEED TO DRAW MORE. BECAUSE...

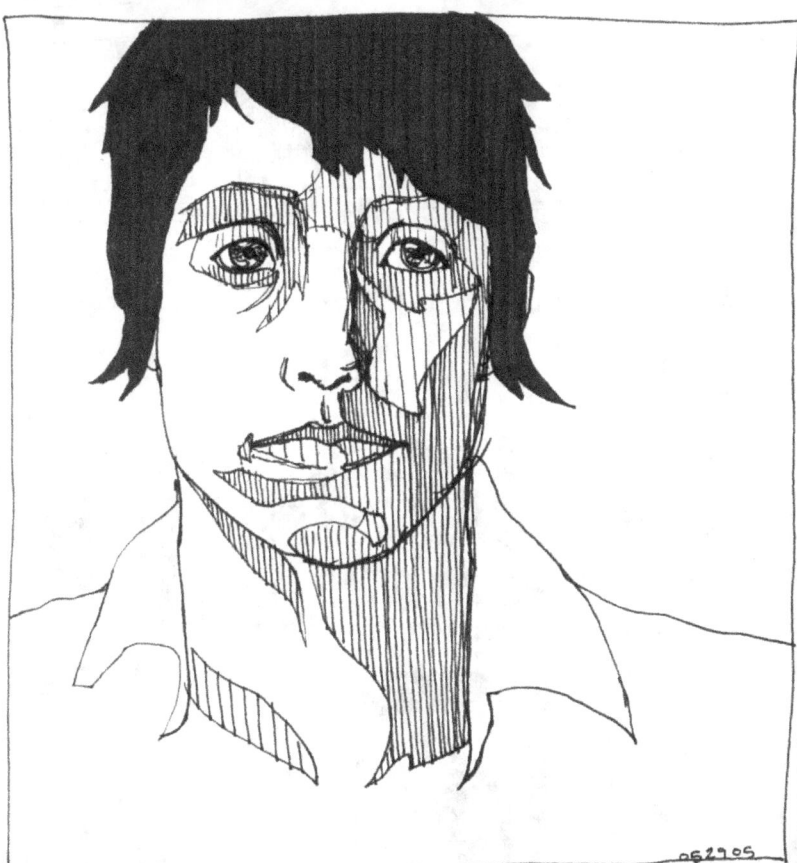

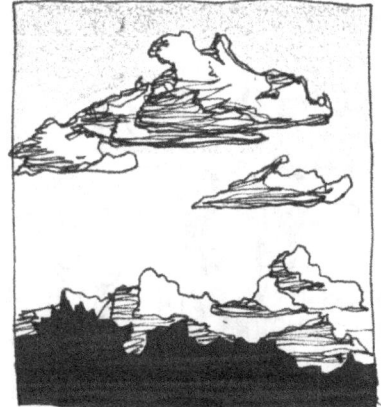

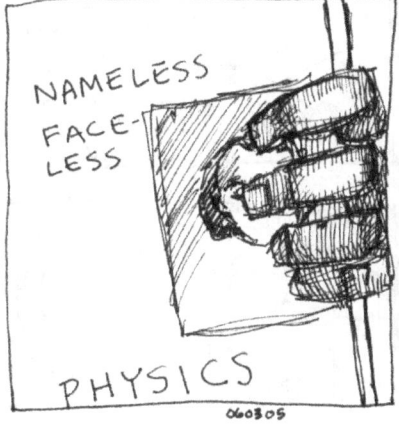

NAMELESS FACE-LESS

PHYSICS

feet slightly touching/ soles and earth solid/ it's new and volant/ this sensation/ of being alone/the daily **bread**

d wait
ing for
poems
i walk
unkno
wn/h
olding
only m
y pur
pose

as i pass everyone by.....
060905

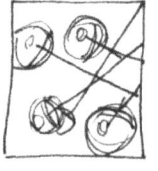 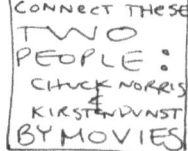 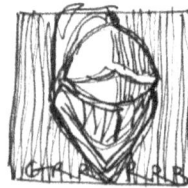 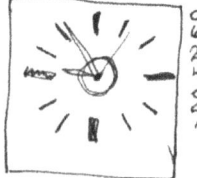
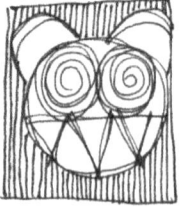 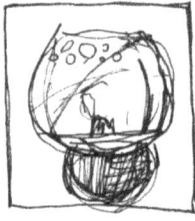 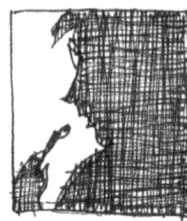 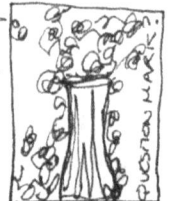

CHAPTER TWO:
THE FIFTH
DIMENSION

ACTUALLY, IT'S CALLED, WAIT, LET ME GET THE BOOK ⟶ THE SECRET OF LIGHT:
VIBRATIONS IN THE FIFTH DIMENSION ︴

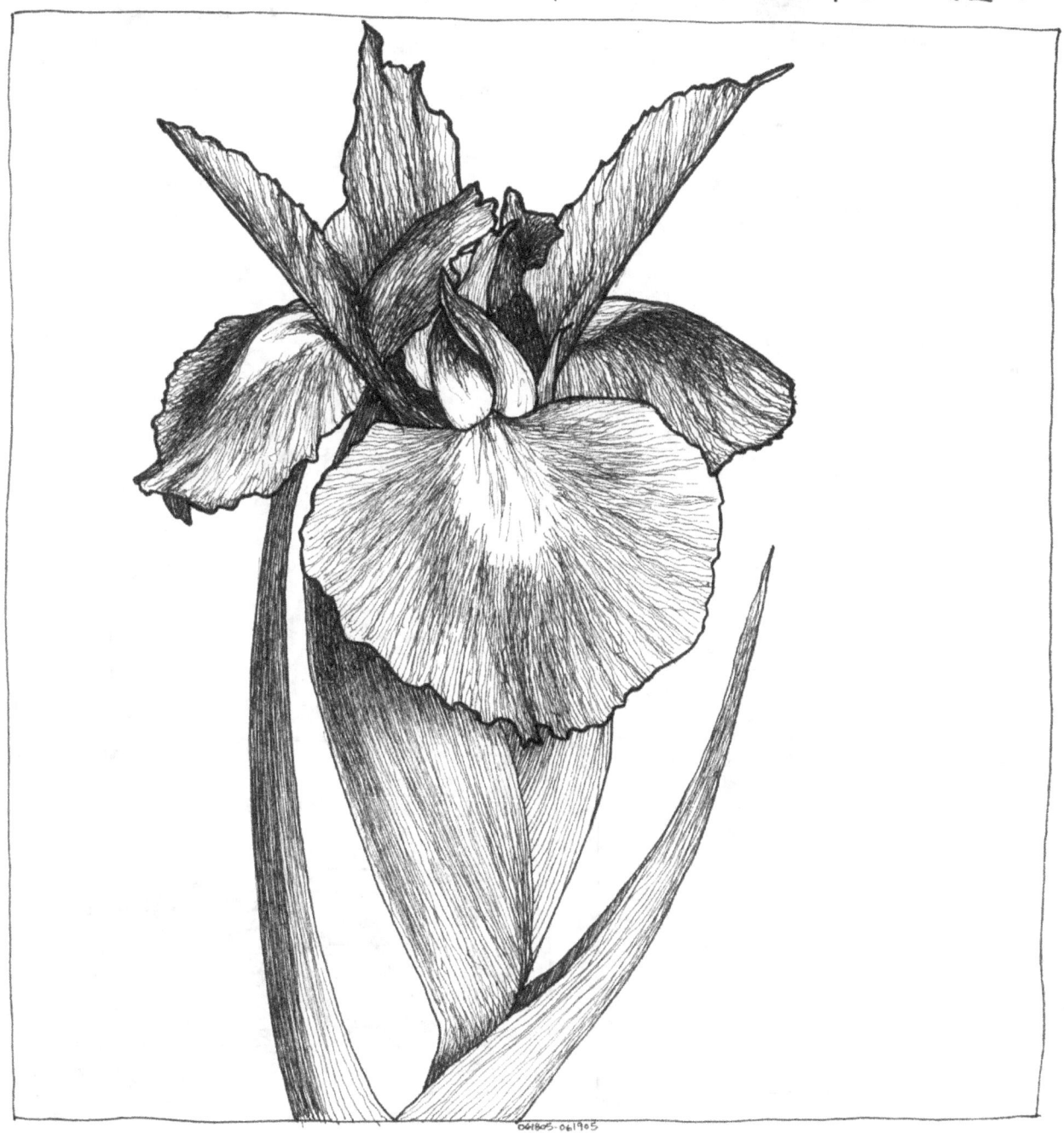

061805-061905

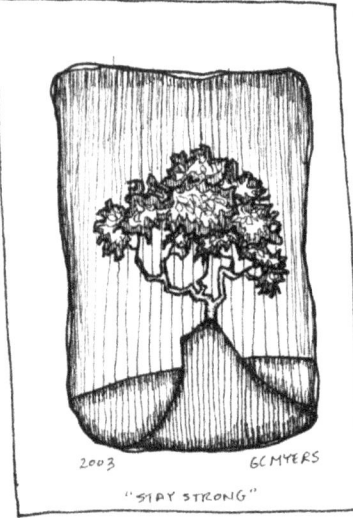

2003   GC MYERS

"STAY STRONG"

WHOEVER YOU ARE: IN THE EVENING STEP OUT
OF YOUR ROOM, WHERE YOU KNOW EVERYTHING;
YOURS IS THE LAST HOUSE BEFORE THE FAR OFF:
WHOEVER YOU ARE,
WITH YOUR EYES, WHICH IN THE WEARINESS
BARELY FREE THEMSELVES FROM THE WORN-OUT THRESHOLD
YOU LIFT VERY SLOWLY ONE BLACK TREE
AND PLACE IT AGAINST THE SKY: SLENDER, ALONE.
AND YOU HAVE MADE THE WORLD. AND IT IS HUGE
AND LIKE A WORD WHICH GROWS RIPE IN SILENCE.
AND AS YOUR WILL SEIZES ON ITS MEANING,
TENDERLY YOUR EYES LET GO . . .

. . . RILKE

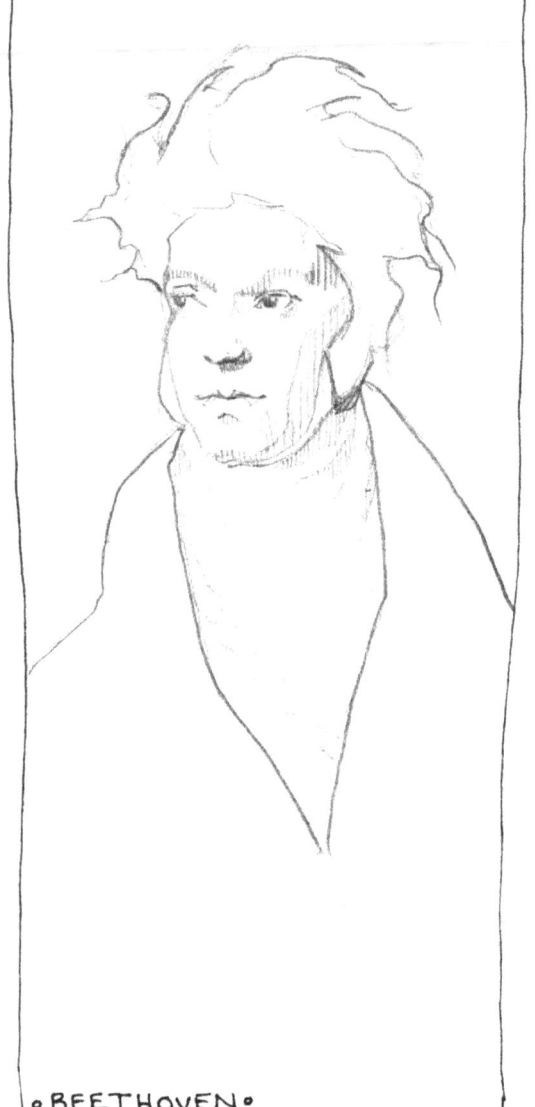

◦BEETHOVEN◦

BY SOMEONE ANONYMOUS

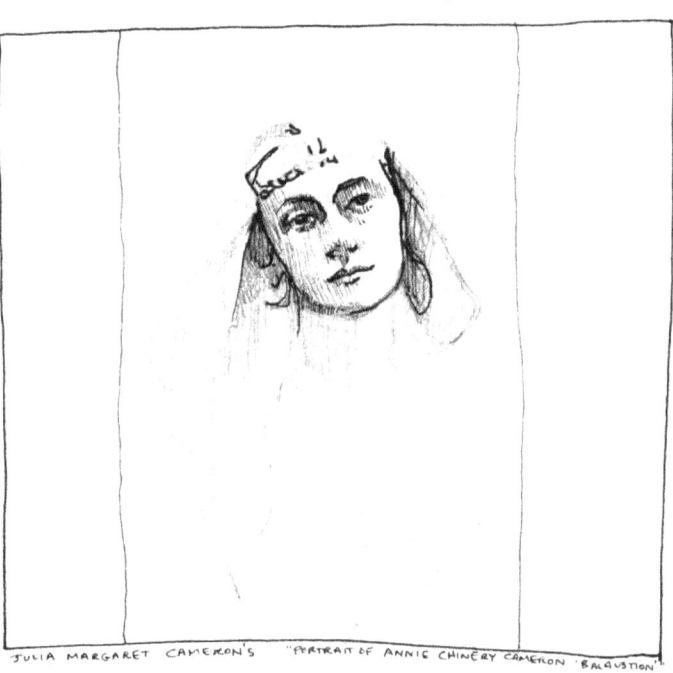

JULIA MARGARET CAMERON'S "PORTRAIT OF ANNIE CHINERY CAMERON 'BALAUSTION'"

WEST END GALLERY

FINE ART

STAPLER

MY BIRTHDAY   08.21.05

BAD

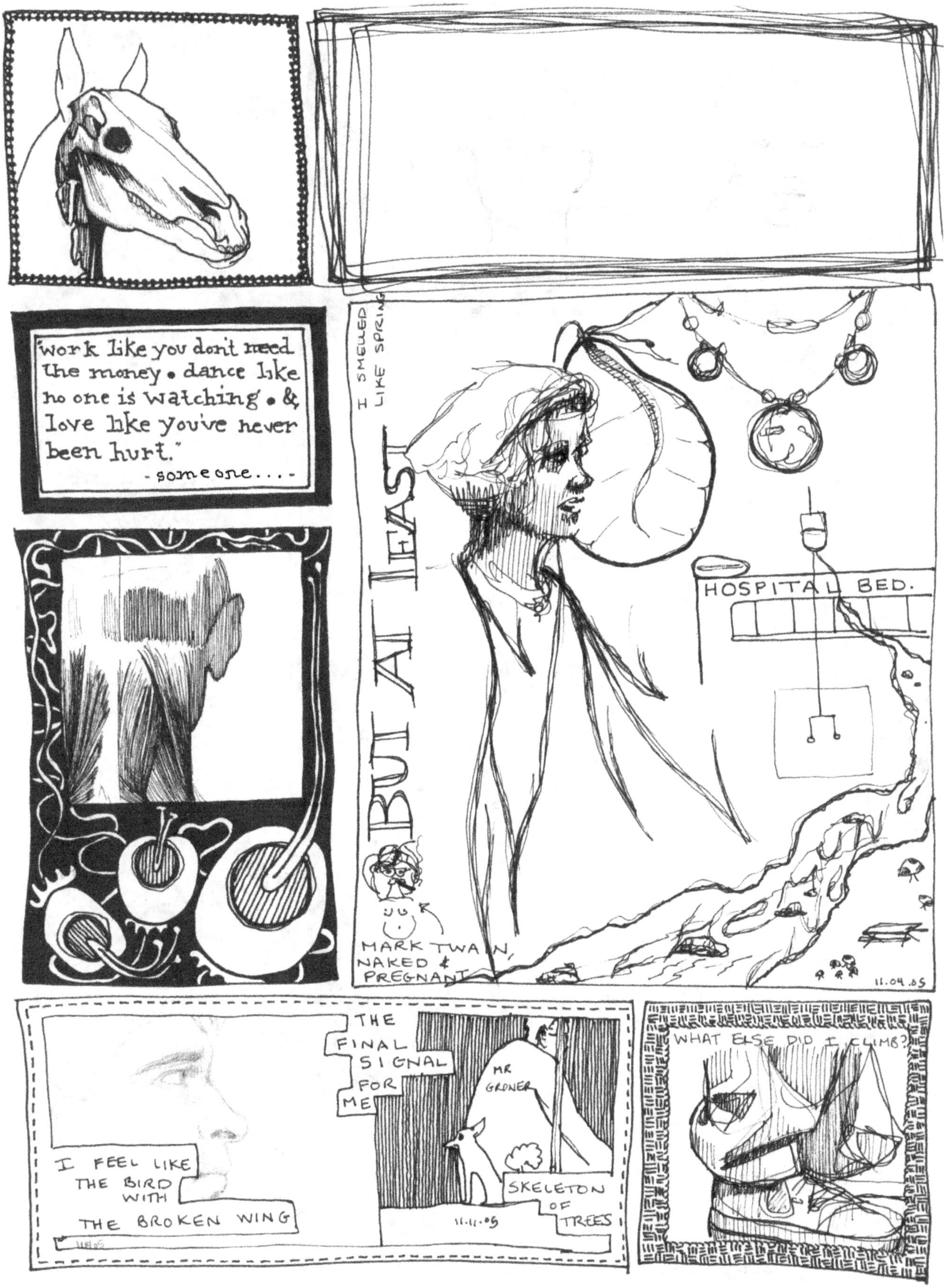

"work like you don't need the money. dance like no one is watching. & love like you've never been hurt."
— some one....

I SMELLED LIKE SPRING

BUT AT LEAST

MARK TWAIN NAKED & PREGNANT

HOSPITAL BED.

11.04.05

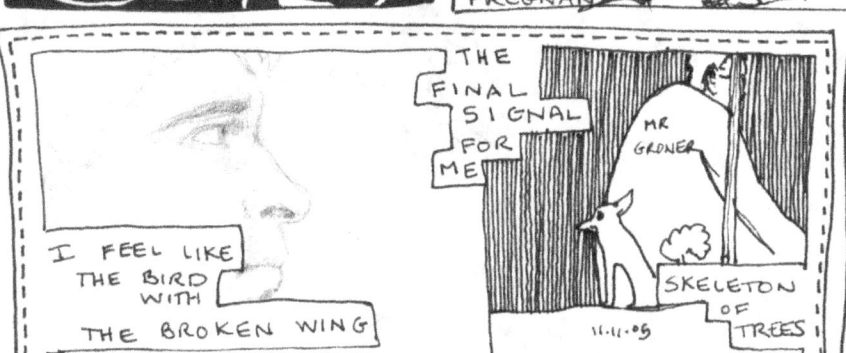

I FEEL LIKE THE BIRD WITH THE BROKEN WING

THE FINAL SIGNAL FOR ME

MR GRONER

SKELETON OF TREES

11.11.05

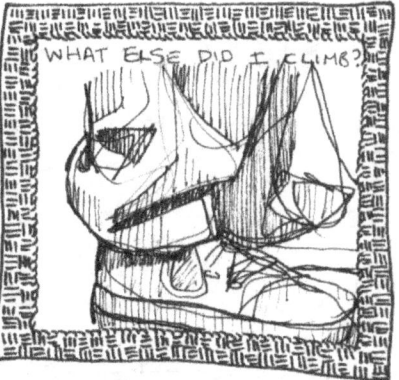

WHAT ELSE DID I CLIMB?

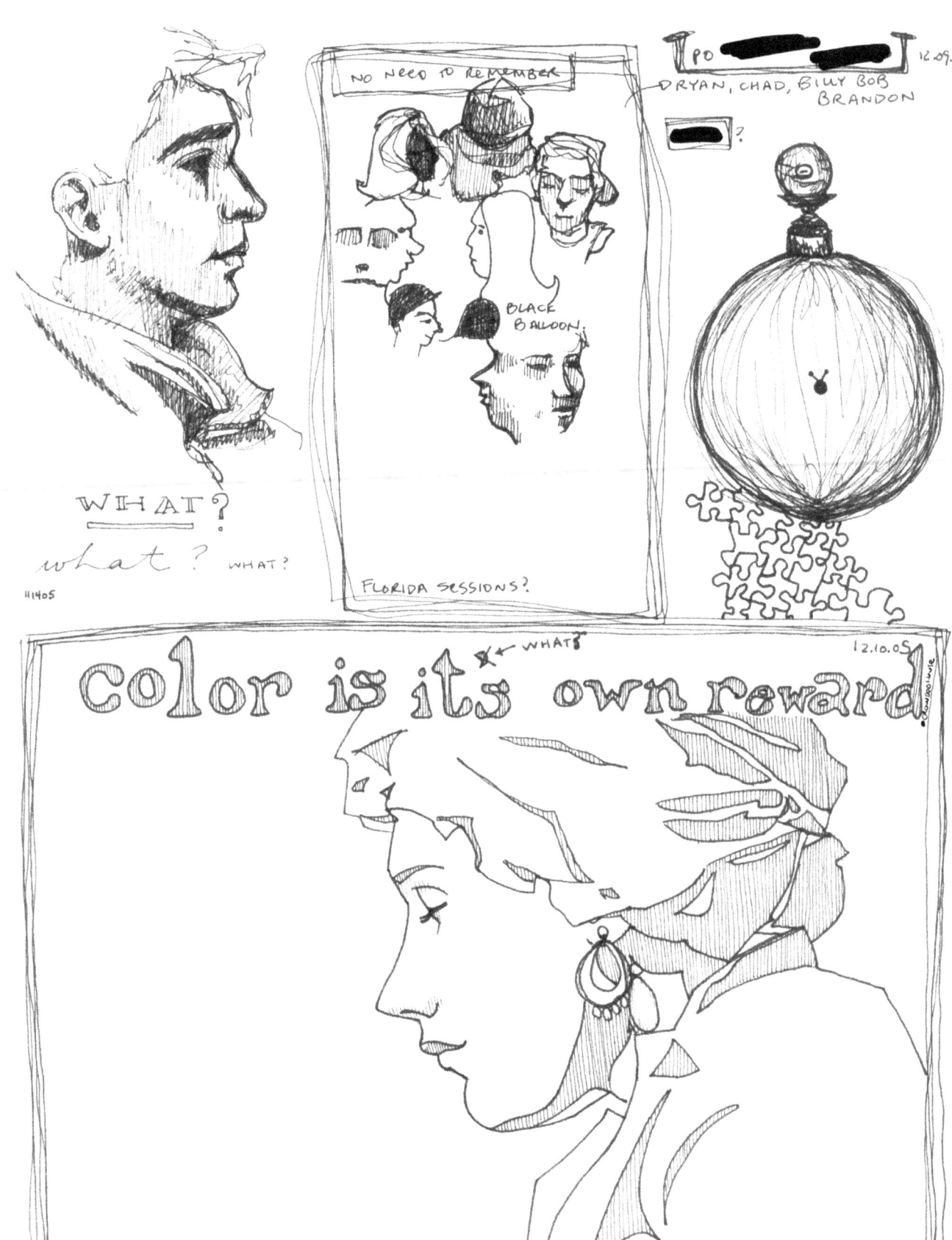

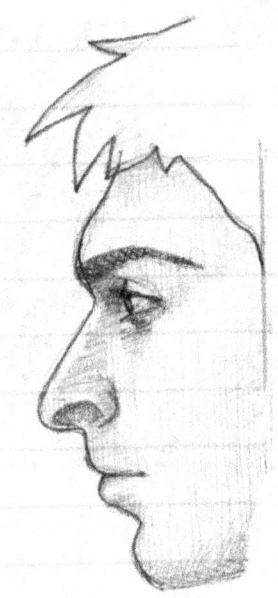

make things big because then it
will look like crap and you
. will learn a lot. 12·14·05

THINGS
DO CHANGE...

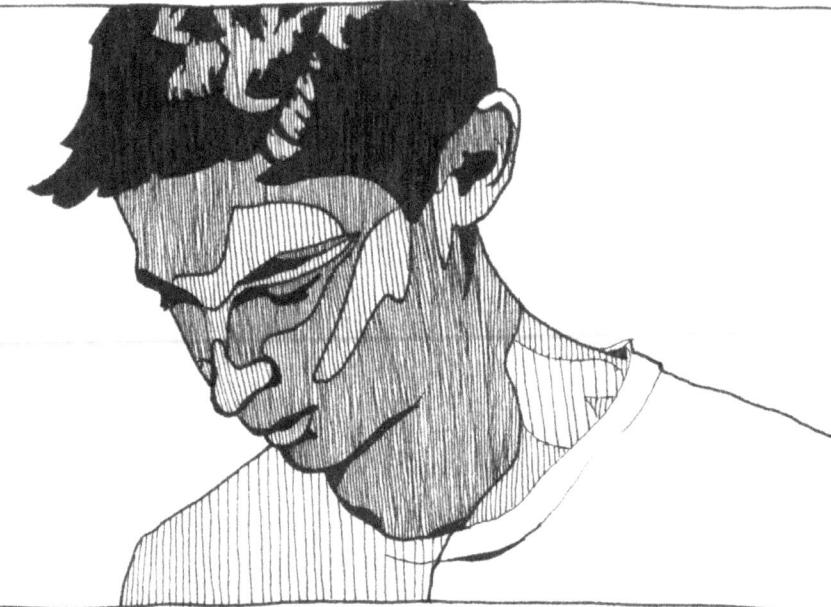

my beautiful
steppenwolf.

finished @ 12:27, 12.14.05

THINGS DO CHANGE THINGS DO CHANGE

THINGS DO CHANGE

THINGS DO CHANGE

CHANGE THINGS DO CHANGE THINGS DO CHANGE

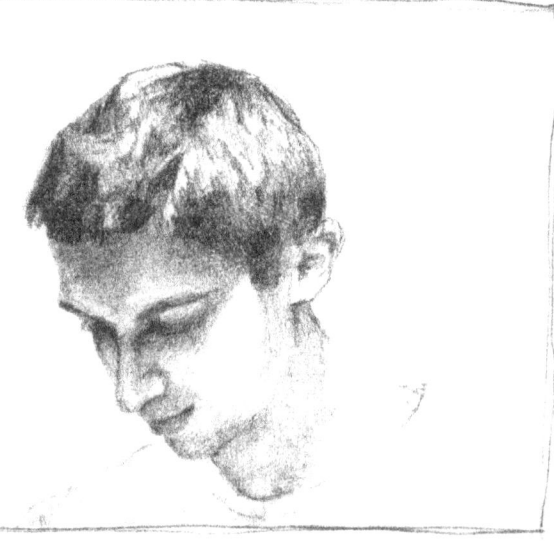

don't worry
everything
ridiculous..

...ryan

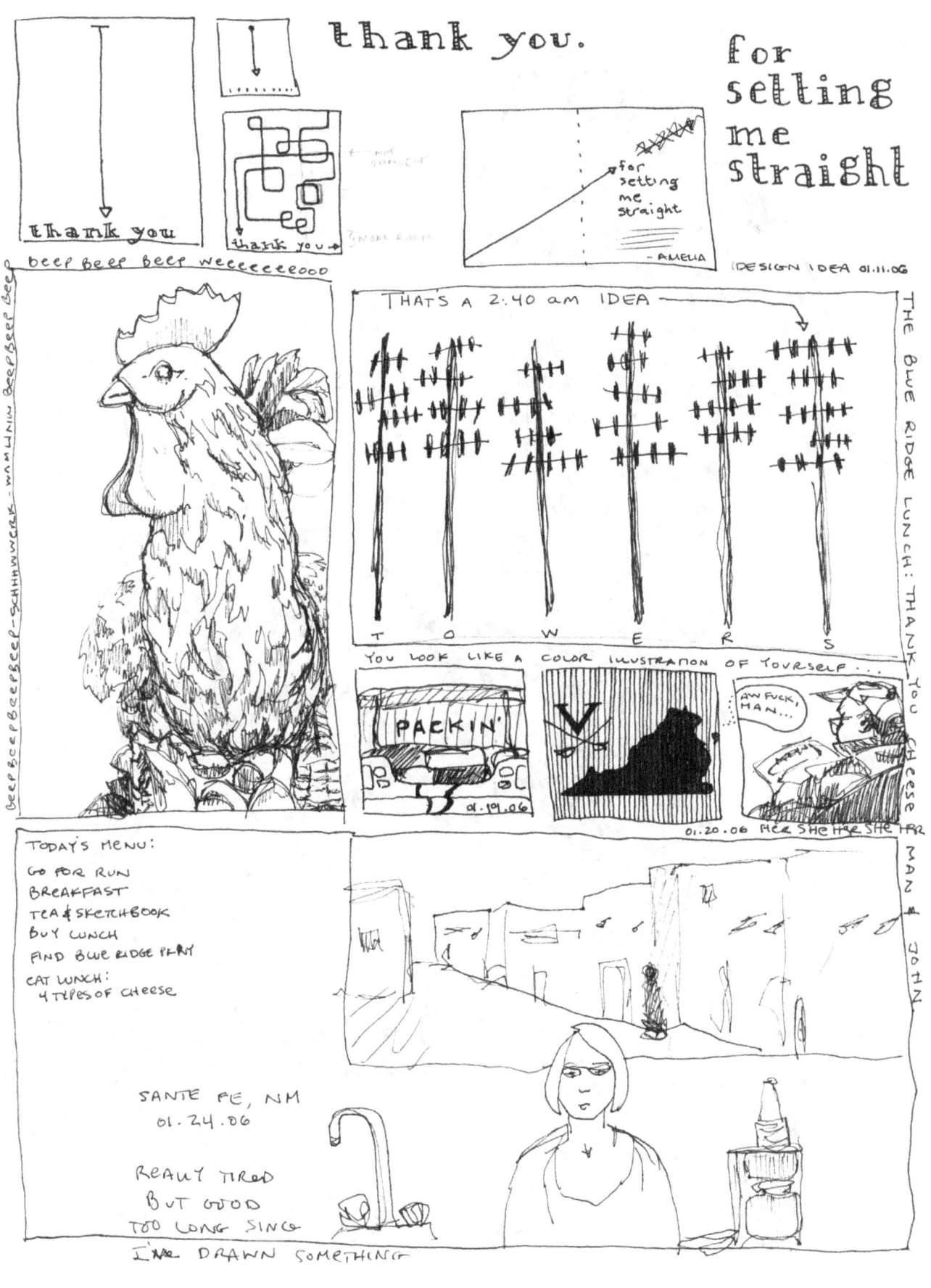

AMELIA HARNAS
ENGLISH CLASS
PAPER ABOUT RYAN
Feb. 15, 2004

RYAN IS OH MY GOD! FREEZING ME.

You are wonderful.

Yes - wonde

You heard me - wonderful.

TO YOU SEEM SO MUCH HAPPIER WHEN YOU'RE ALONE. AND NOW I'M DEBATING WHETHER OR NOT I SHOULD SEND THIS TO YOU. SURE. WHAT THE HELL. WE ALL LOVE HONESTY RIGHT? I FEEL LIKE I'M LOSING MY MIND. I'M JUST GOING TO GO SOAK IN THE SHOWER NOW. SORRY ABOUT THE OTHER PHONE MESSAGE.
OK
AND I KNOW YOU DON'T UNDERSTAND IT WHEN I GET THIS WAY. I DON'T EXPECT YOU TO UNDERSTAND. I THINK THE BEST THING YOU CAN DO IN THESE SITUATIONS IS TO JUST HOLD ME AND LET ME GET IT OUT. BUT I'M ALONE NOW ... SO I'M JUST GOING TO HAVE TO DEAL WITH IT.

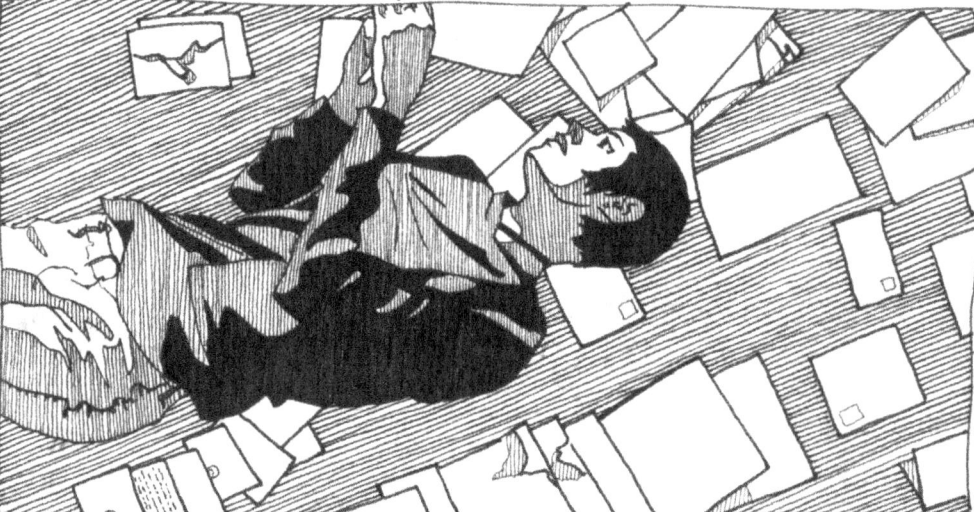

3, yes. Make me immortal dearest
And I shall likewise cast your name
Within these very words; that when
he world of your deft hand shall be
pon a newly-cresting wave, the pearl
of some old oyster found half sunk,
Among the shell-less sand a sleepless
mmanding of the sea, a jeweled ch
t do not fret, for those of future ti
Shall find herein no blemish of you
mockery shall here beset your prime,
Nor will a doubtful glare on you be ca
nder Apollo's seal and lyric chime

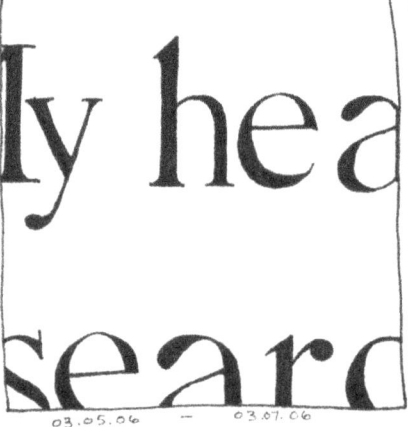

ly hea

searc

you will with each new wav
be forever last. you will wit
h each new wave forever las
t. you will with each new wav
e forever last. you will with
each new wave forever last.
you will with each new wave
forever last. you will with
each new wave forever las
t. you will with each new w
ave forever last. you will wit
h each new wave forever last.
you will with each new wave
forever last. you will with each
new wave forever last. you wi
ll with each new wave foreve
r last. you will with each
new wave forever last

03.05.06 — 03.07.06

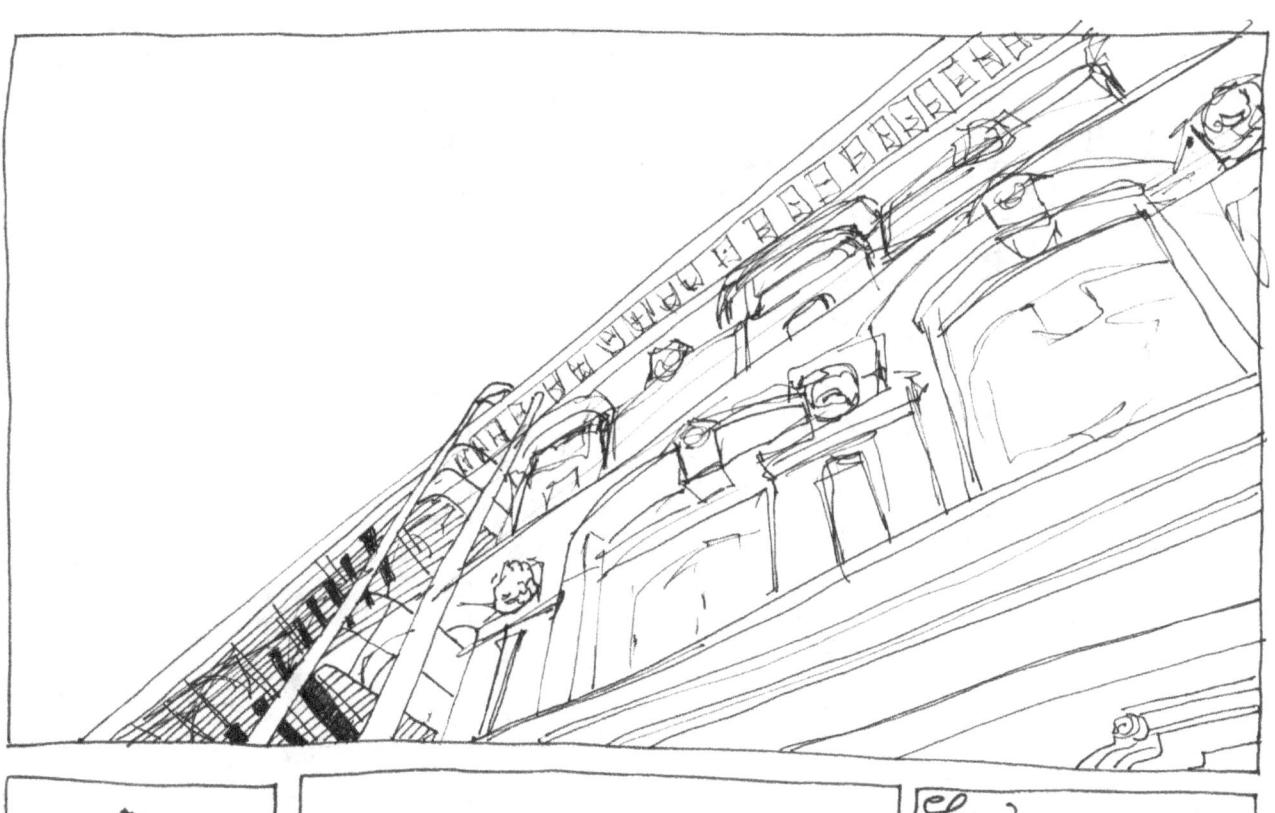

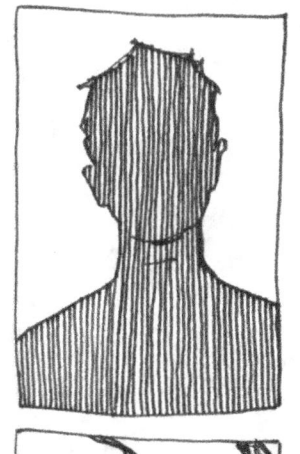

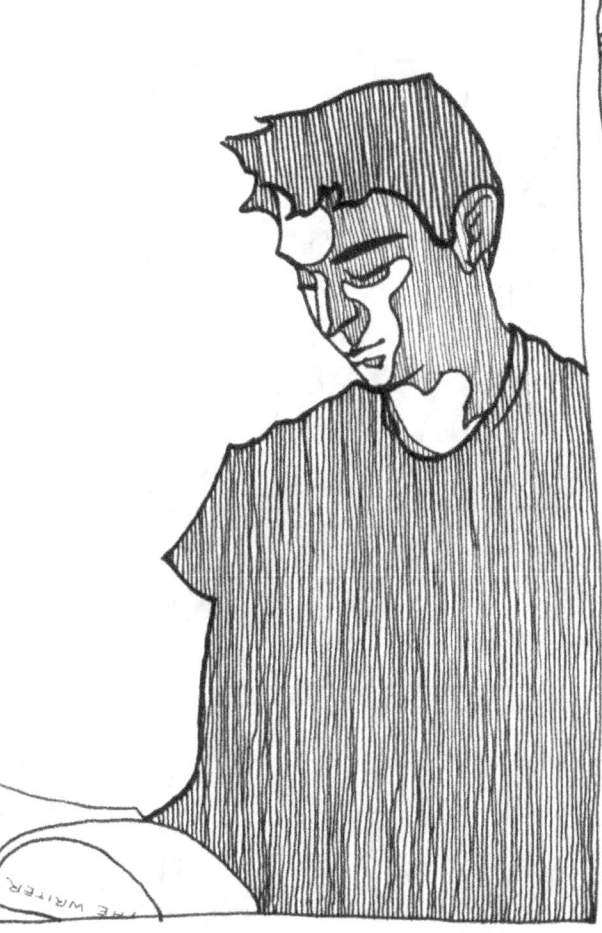

In dreams at night, I hold you in my arms, or follow in your flight across the Martian field, or pursue through yielding waves the boy who will not yield. —Horace

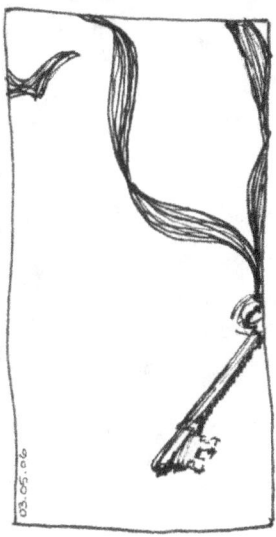

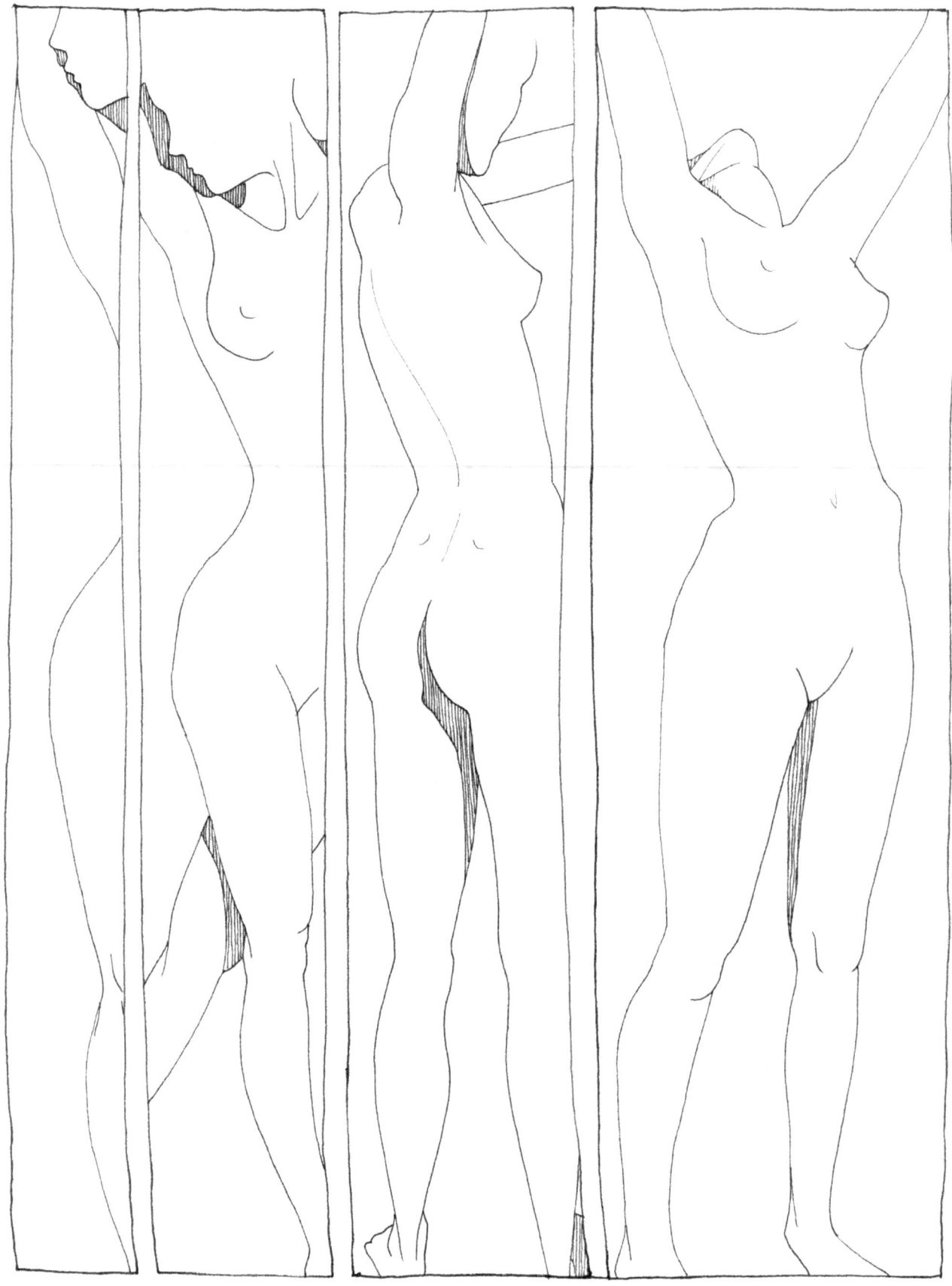

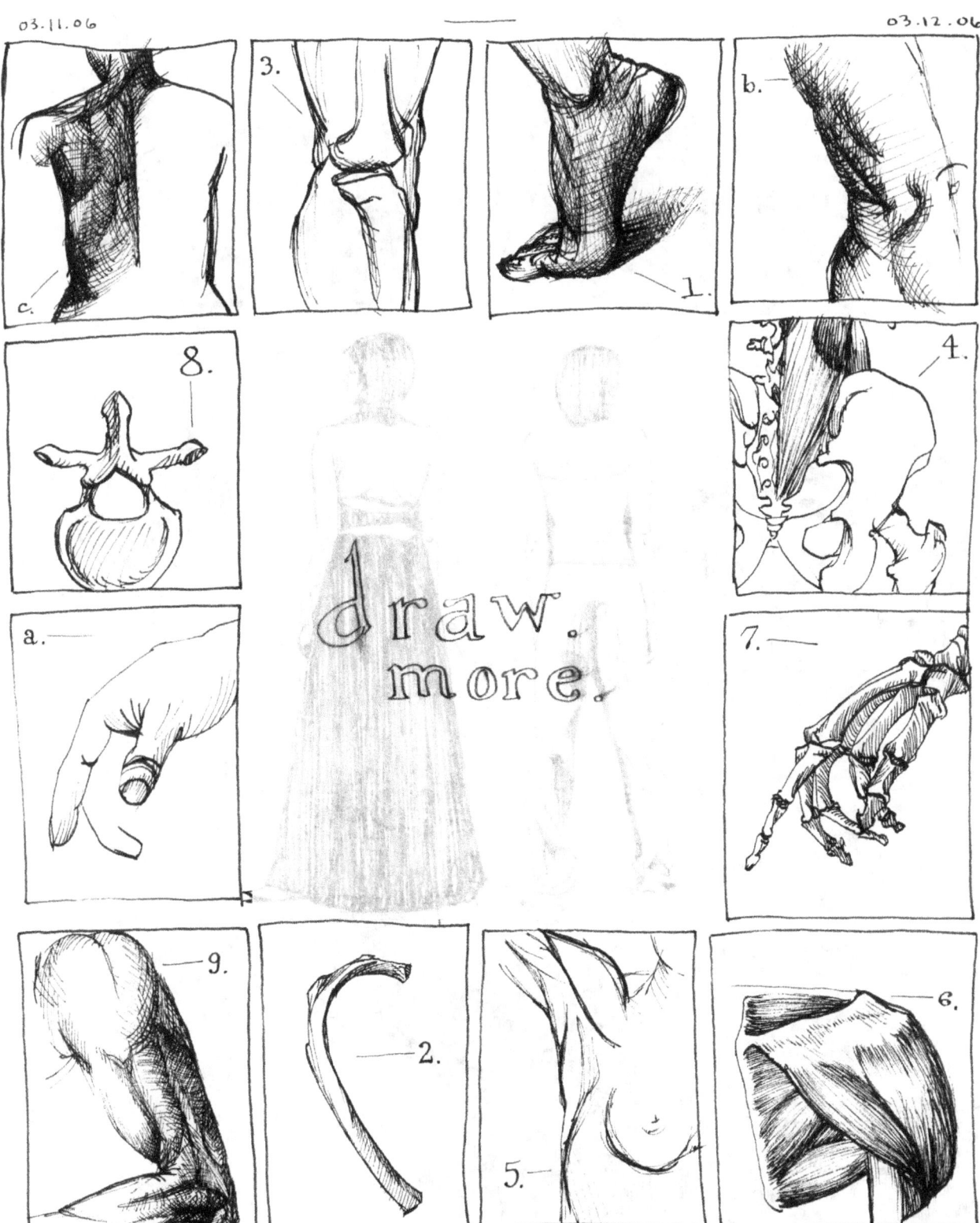

draw.
more.

Both connoisseurs and artists are rediscovering the rewards and pleasures of drawing, the activity which Cennino Cennini in the fourteenth century considered "both the necessary foundation of practice for all and a natural intellectual inclination of the talented." Only a generation ago drawing as it had been practiced in the past seem-

— D.M.M

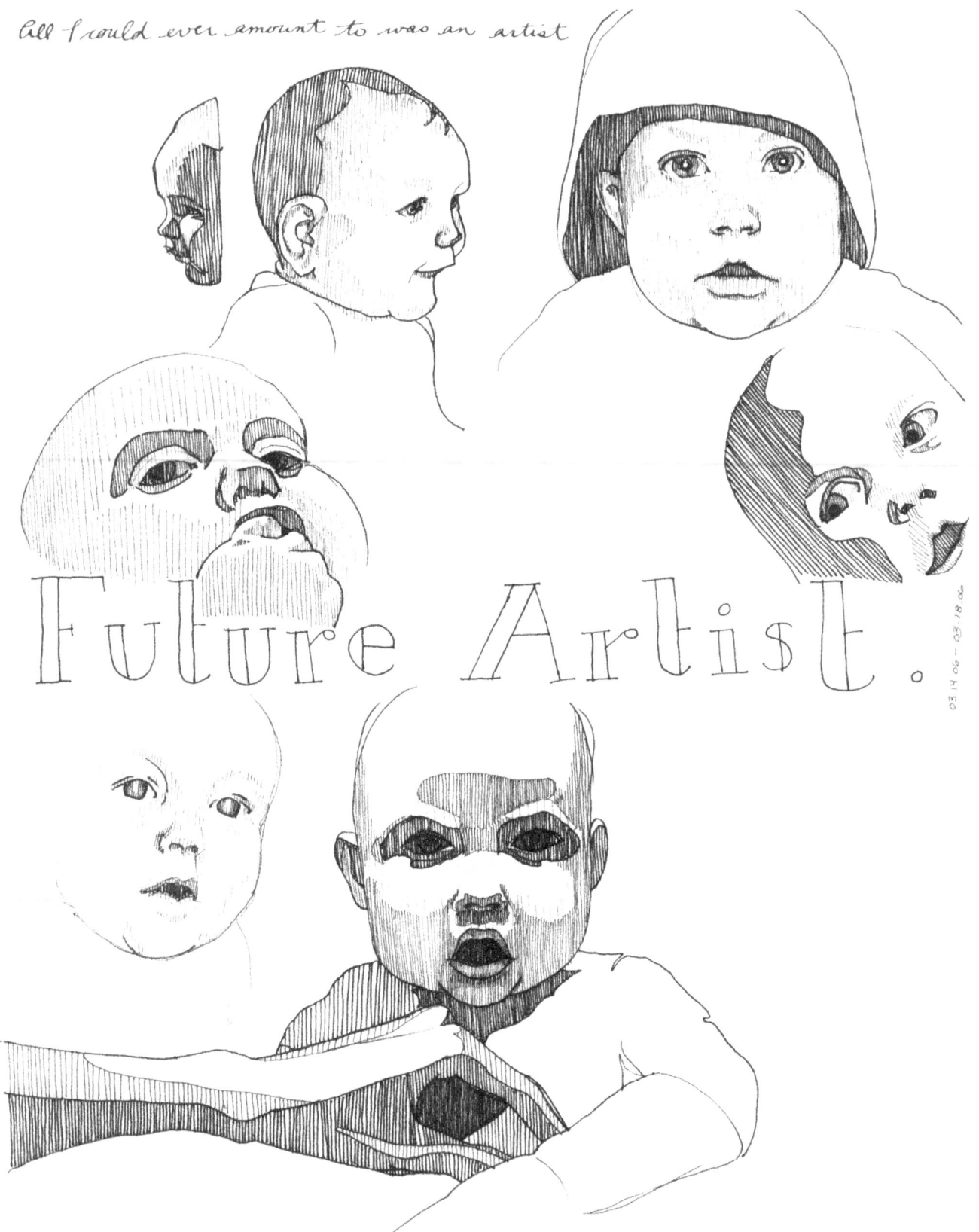

All I could ever amount to was an artist

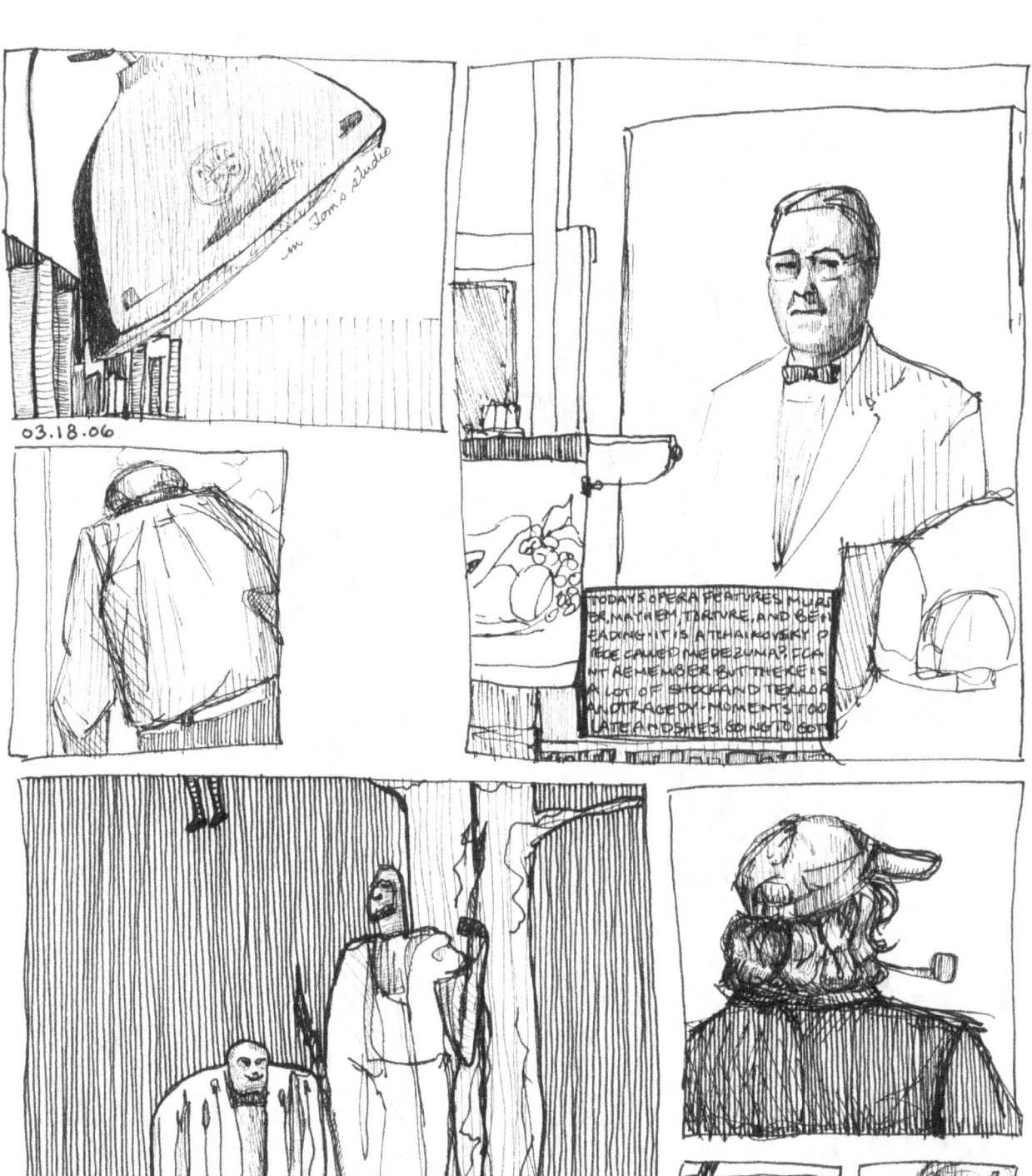

03.18.06

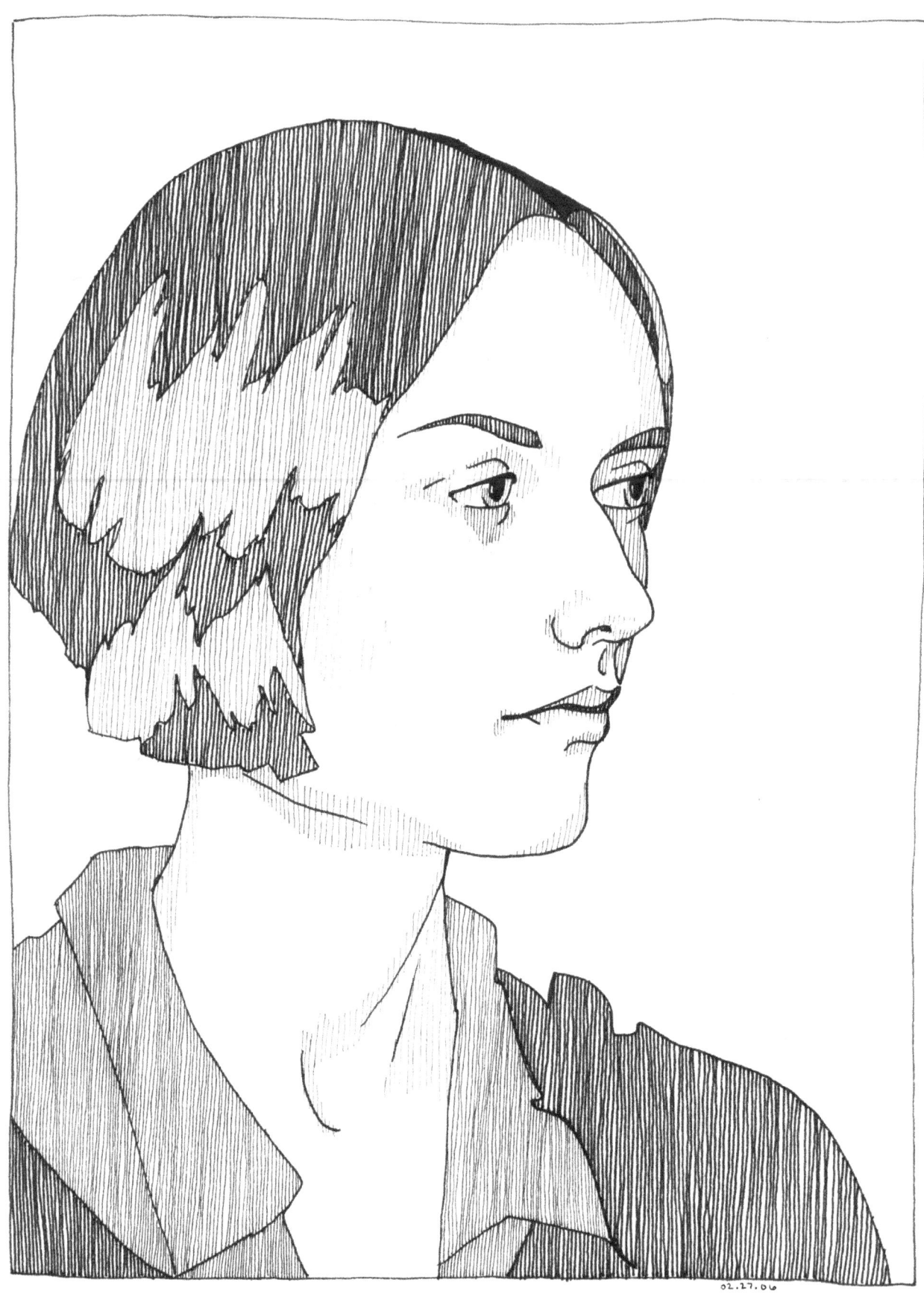

02.27.06

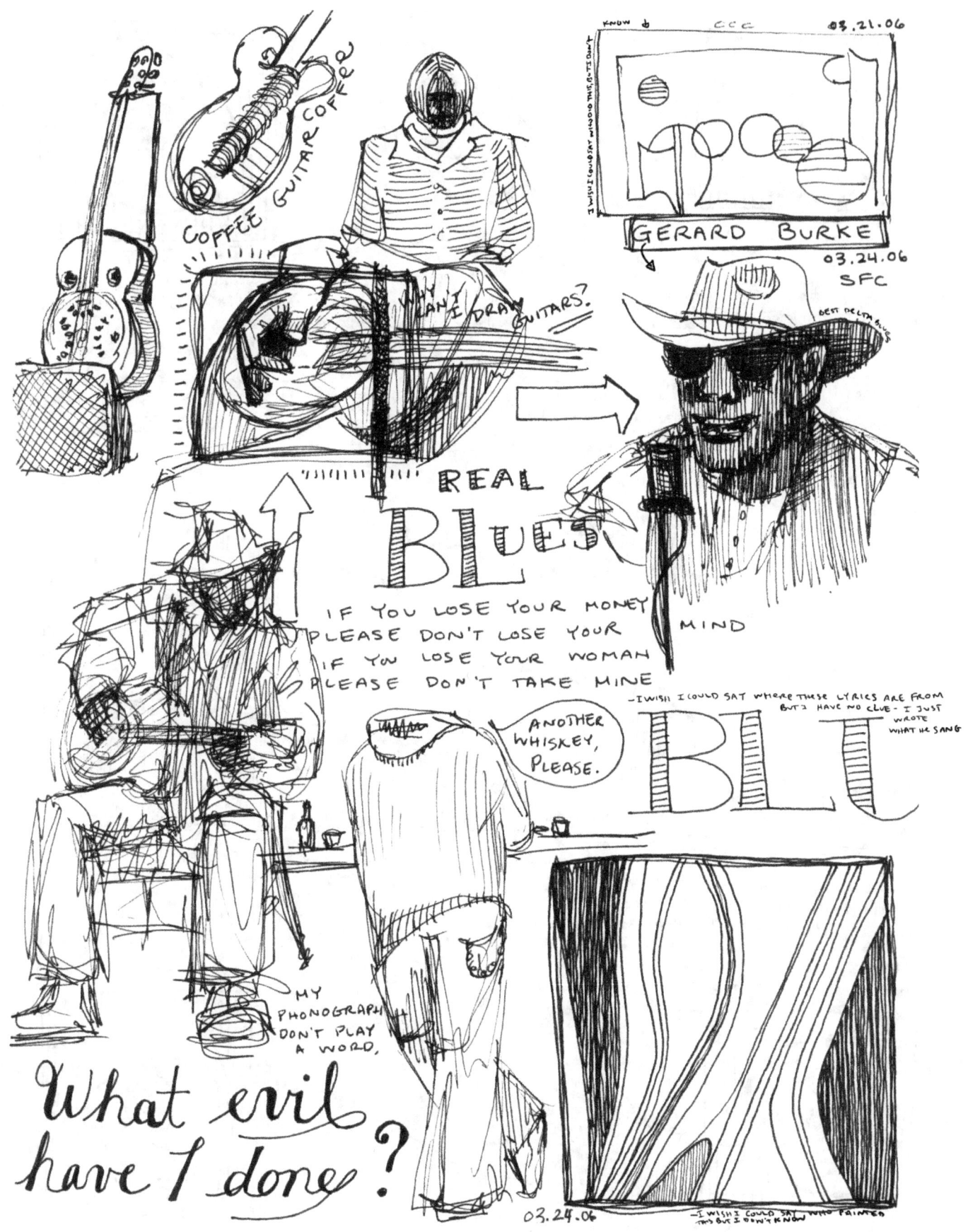

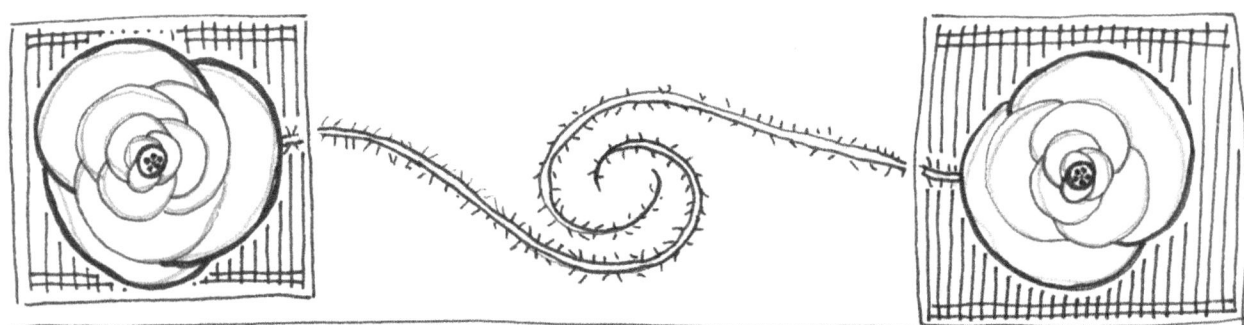

TIPTOE AROUND DROWNING WORMS BRANCHES IN HALOS AROUND ORANGE LAMP LIGHT LAST YEAR THIS YEAR NEXT YEAR SORE FINGERS FROM SONGS ON STRINGS A LONELY HOLLOW VOICE AN INFINITE IN BETWEEN WHAT YOU DO AND WHAT YOU CHOOSE DO NOT LOCK THE DOOR ONNY PINK TENDRILS STRETCHING ACROSS CONCRETE IN SPRING RAIN INCHING TOWARDS ROAD UNDER FEET UNDER WHEELS EMERGE ONLY TO DROWN OR GET TRAMPLED GREASE AND DIRTY GLASSES BANDANA COVERING MATTED HAIR PENCIL SKETCHES TRYT TO BE GOOD AT SOMETHING BE AN ARTIST TIME GOES BY SO SLOWLY AND TIME CAN DO SO MUCH ARE YOU STILL MINE I NEED YOU LOVE LONELY RIVERS FLOW TO THE SEAS WAIT FOR ME I'LL BE COMING HOME WAIT FOR ME OH MY LOVE MY DARLING I HUNGER FOR YOUR TOUCH AND WHAT AM I DOING IN THIS YEAR WITHOUT MEN IS IT ACTUALLY WORKING IT'S THE SAYING THAT IF IT DOESN'T BRING YOU ALIVE, IT IS TOO SMALL FOR YOU I WONDER WHAT SONG WILL COME ON NEXT GOOD OLD SCHUMANN HIS FIRST SYMPHONY I BELIEVE I NEED TO DRAW MORE THE PROPORTIONS ARENT RIGHT YET WHICH IS A MAJOR PROBLEM DOES THAT MEAN THAT I JUST KEEP DRAWING?

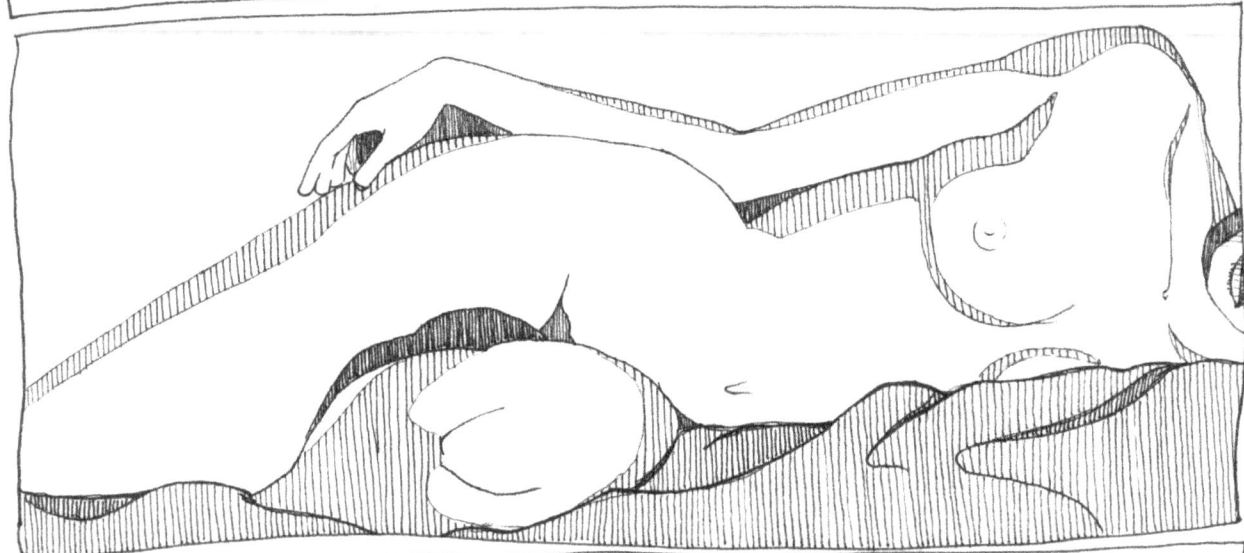

I NEED TO DO MORE STUDIES OF FABRIC AND DRAPERY LOOKING BACK AT THIS DRAWING IT'S NOT SO BAD, BUT I'M SURE IN A FEW DAYS IT WILL LOOK POSITIVELY AWFUL GO GO GO OR RUN RUN RUN. IT ISN'T THAT BAD AT ALL AND THEN I'LL FINISH THAT OTHER PAGE OF SKETCHES THAT I STARTED AT ALFRED MAYBE I'LL GO TO SOULFULL CUP TO FINISH THAT PAGE AND WHICH WHAT? I MEANT TO SAY THAT DRAWING IS GOOD BUT I'M GETTING ANTSY TO START PAINTING AGAIN IN BOTH WATER COLOR AND OIL AND I NEED TO READ FOR CLASSES AND SUCH WHICH I CAN'T WAIT TO GET IT OVER WITH AND HAVE MY DEGREE IT'S COMING IT'S COMING I SWEAR I CAN DO IT AND PULL IT OFF SOON BUT MAYBE THE LESSON I NEED TO LEARN IS TO BE PATIENT AND FOLLOW THROUGH TO GET IT DONE THAT'S A REALLY LONG ARM WITH A SMALL HAND I NEED TO PAINT AGAIN AND BE GOOD AT SOMETHING AGAIN WHAT IS THIS FEARFUL SITTING AROUND AND PROCRASTINATING CRAP I NEED TO STOP AND BE DONE WITH AND I NEED TO CHALLENGE MYSELF

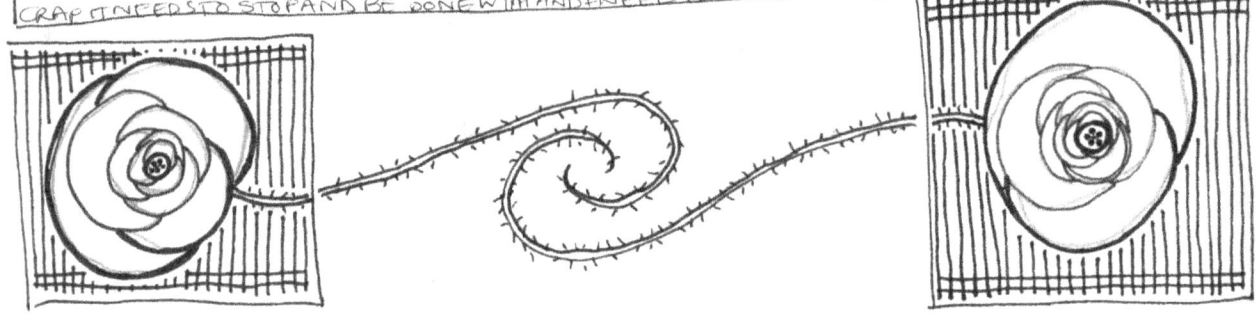

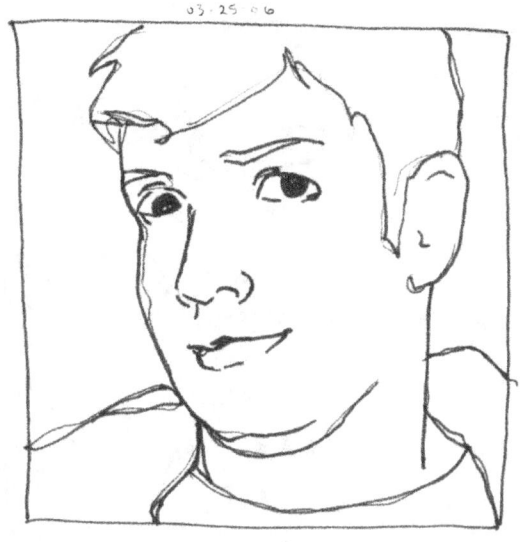

03.25.06

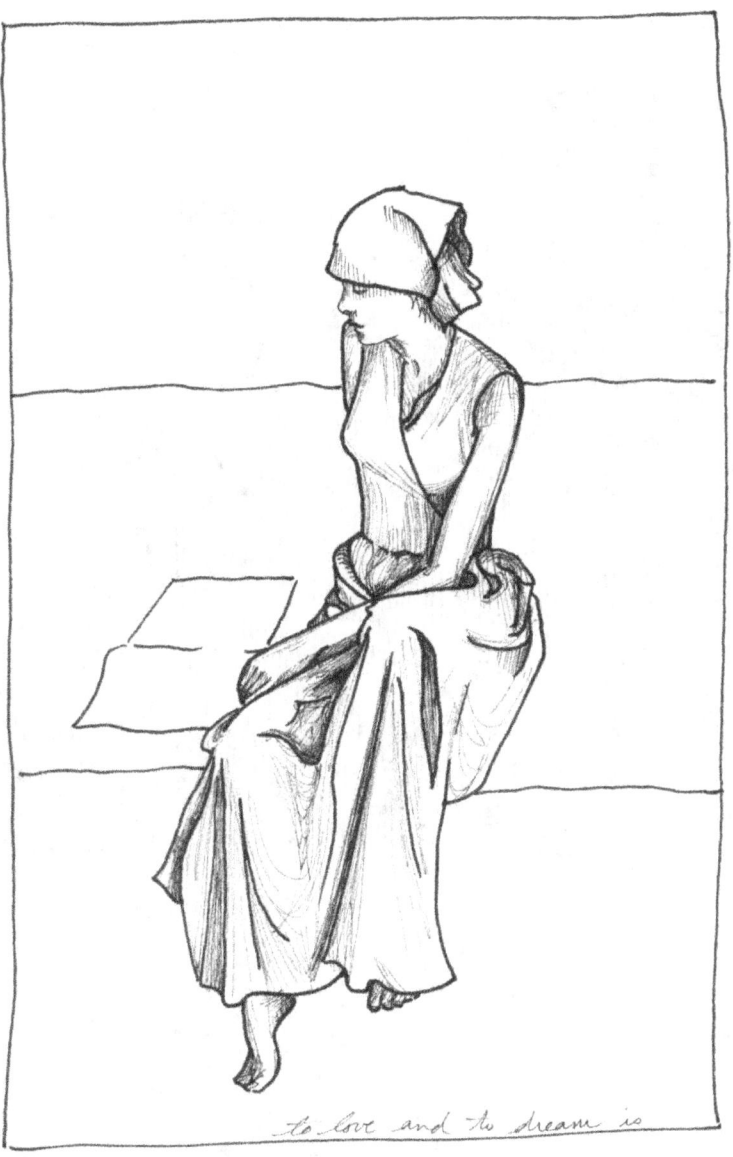

to love and to dream is

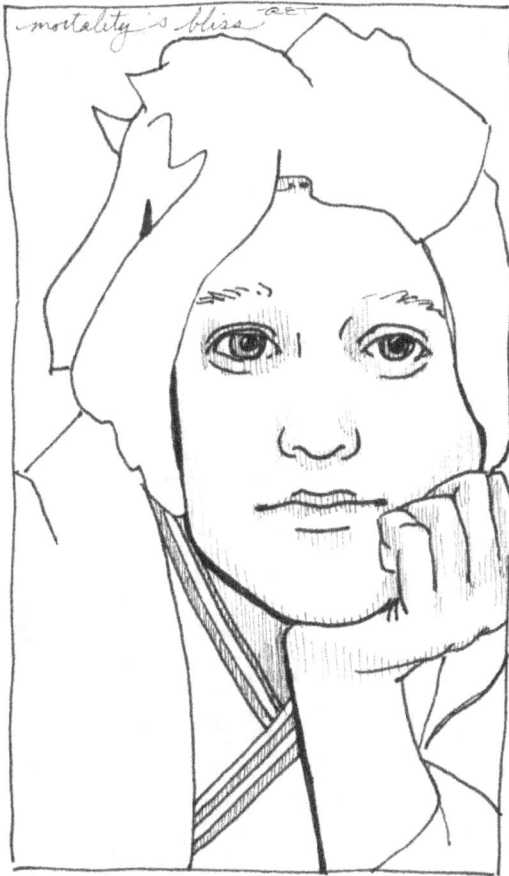

mortality is bliss

all the time, I'll know...

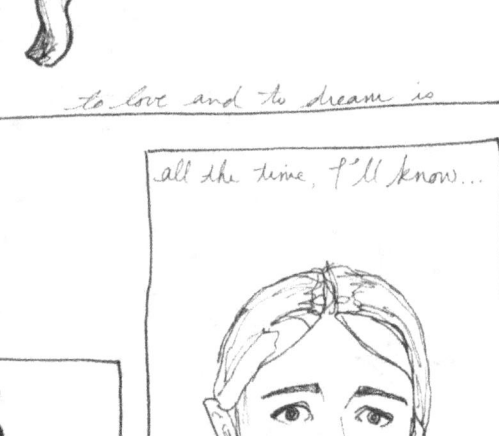

Le chat

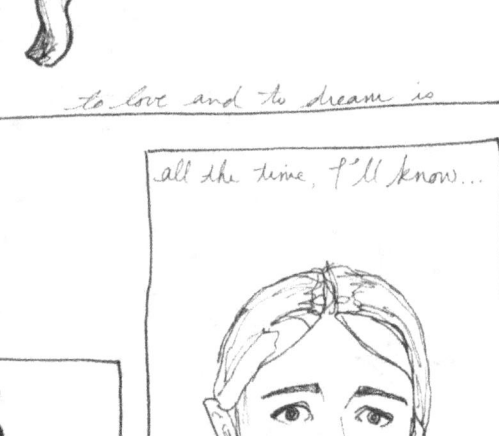

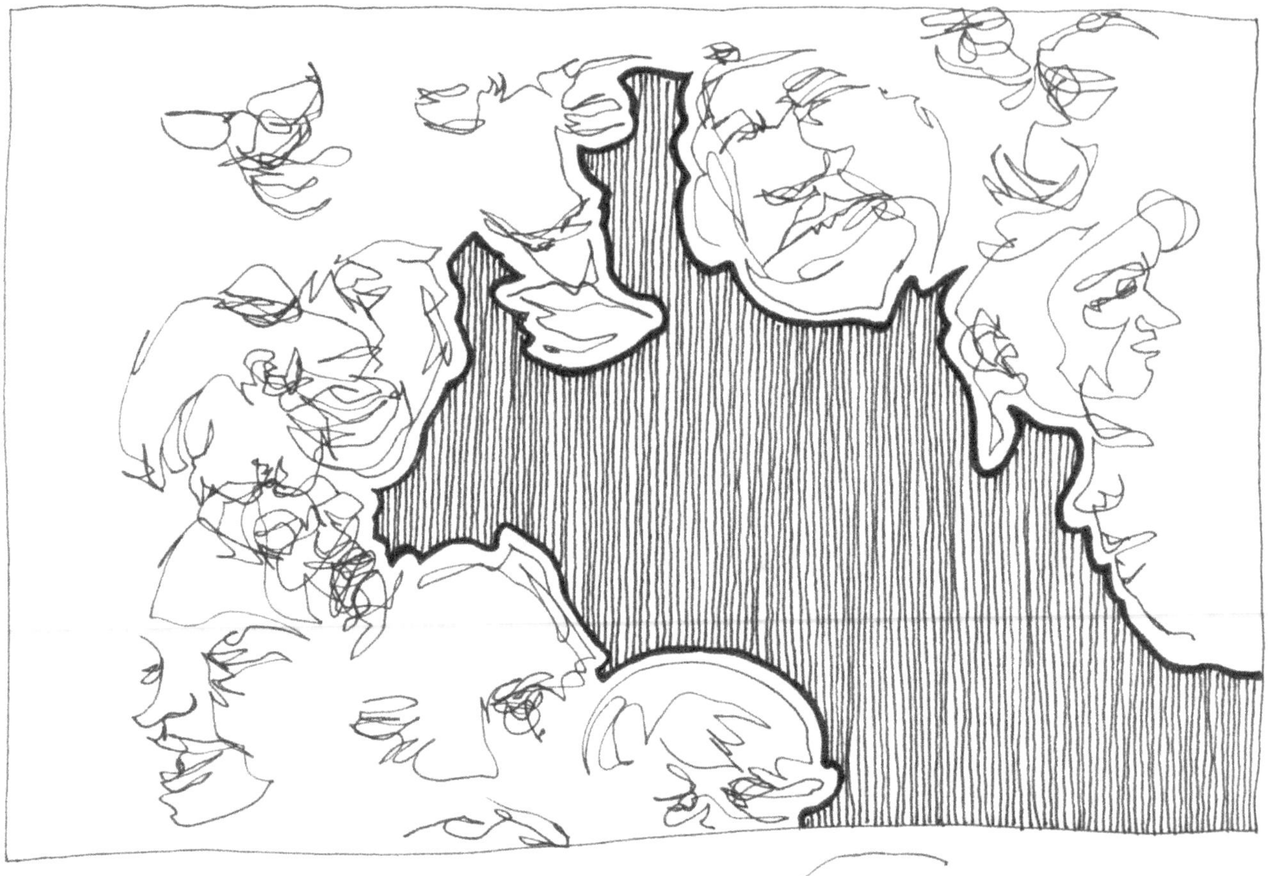

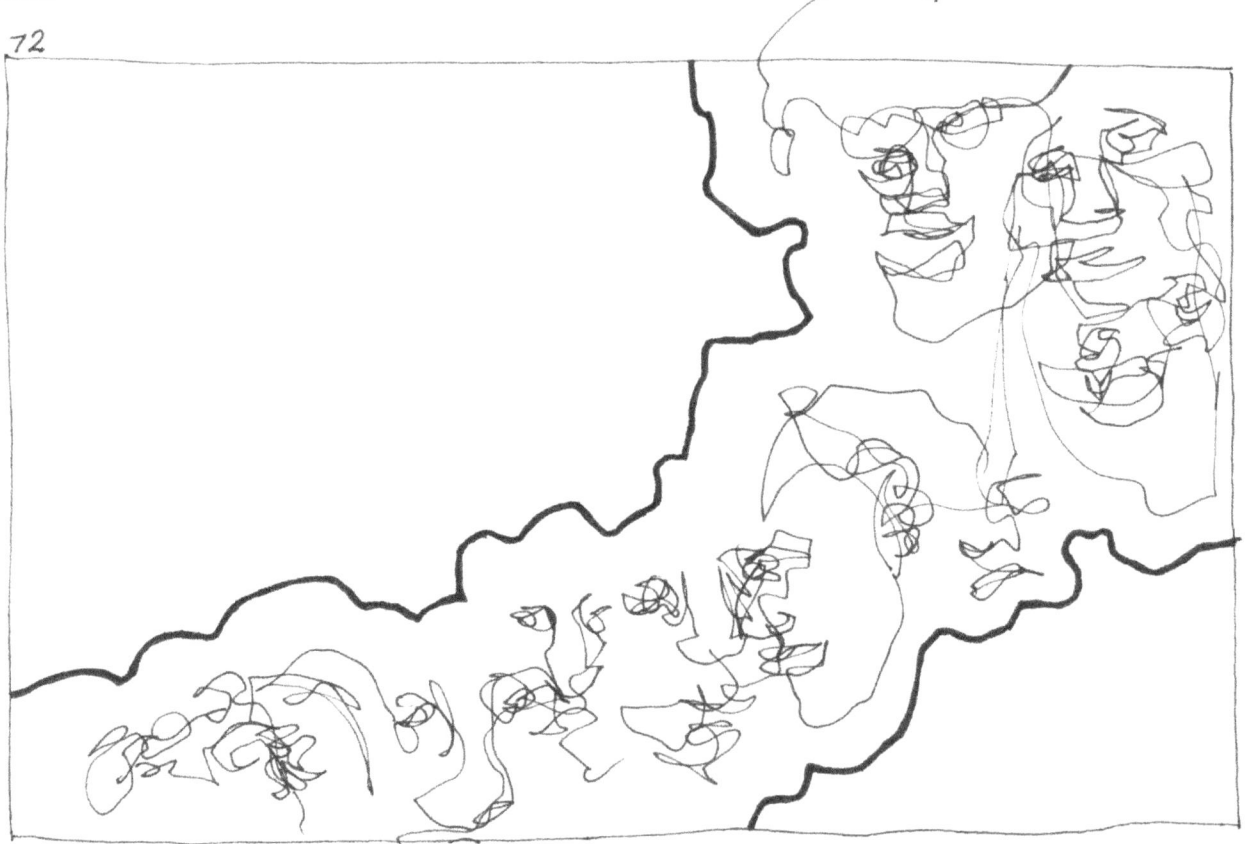

72

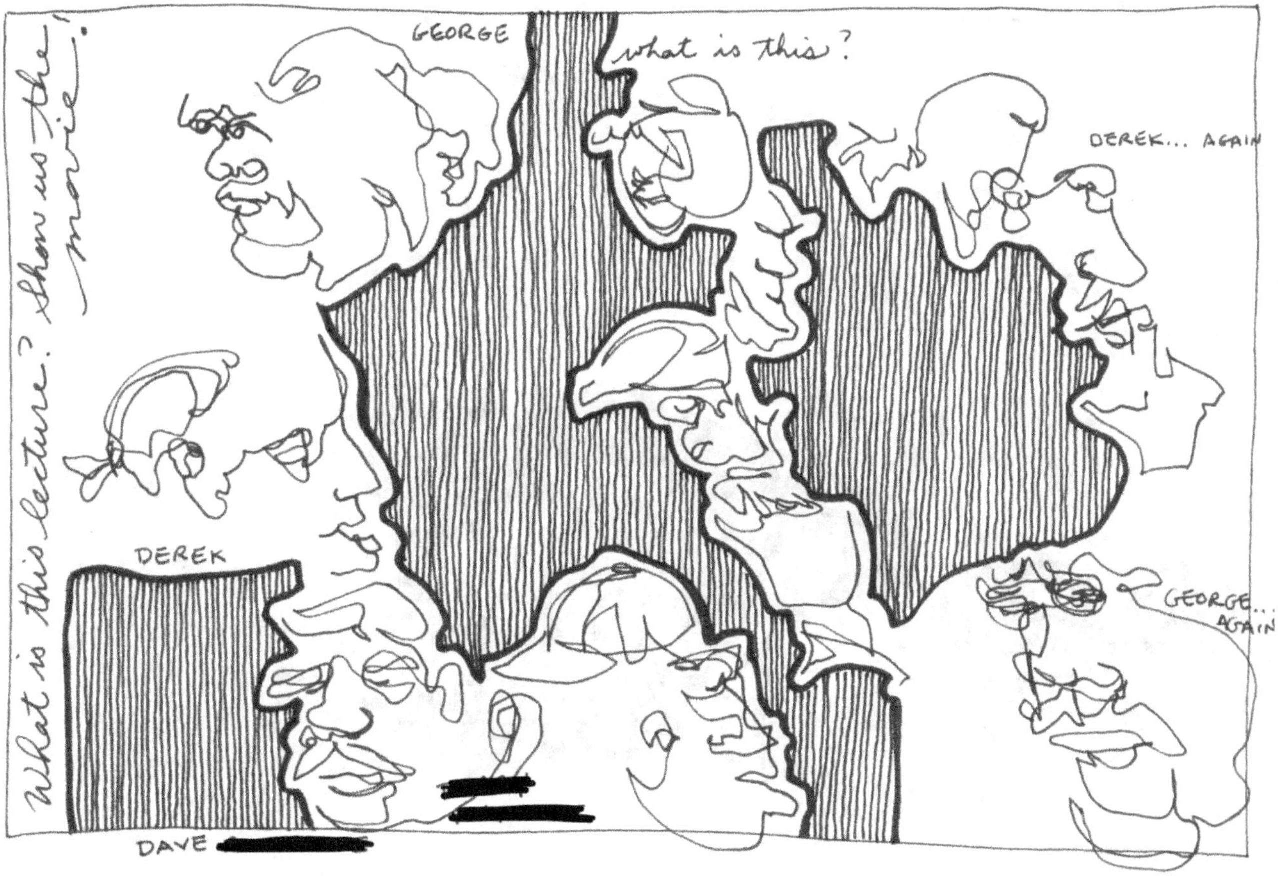

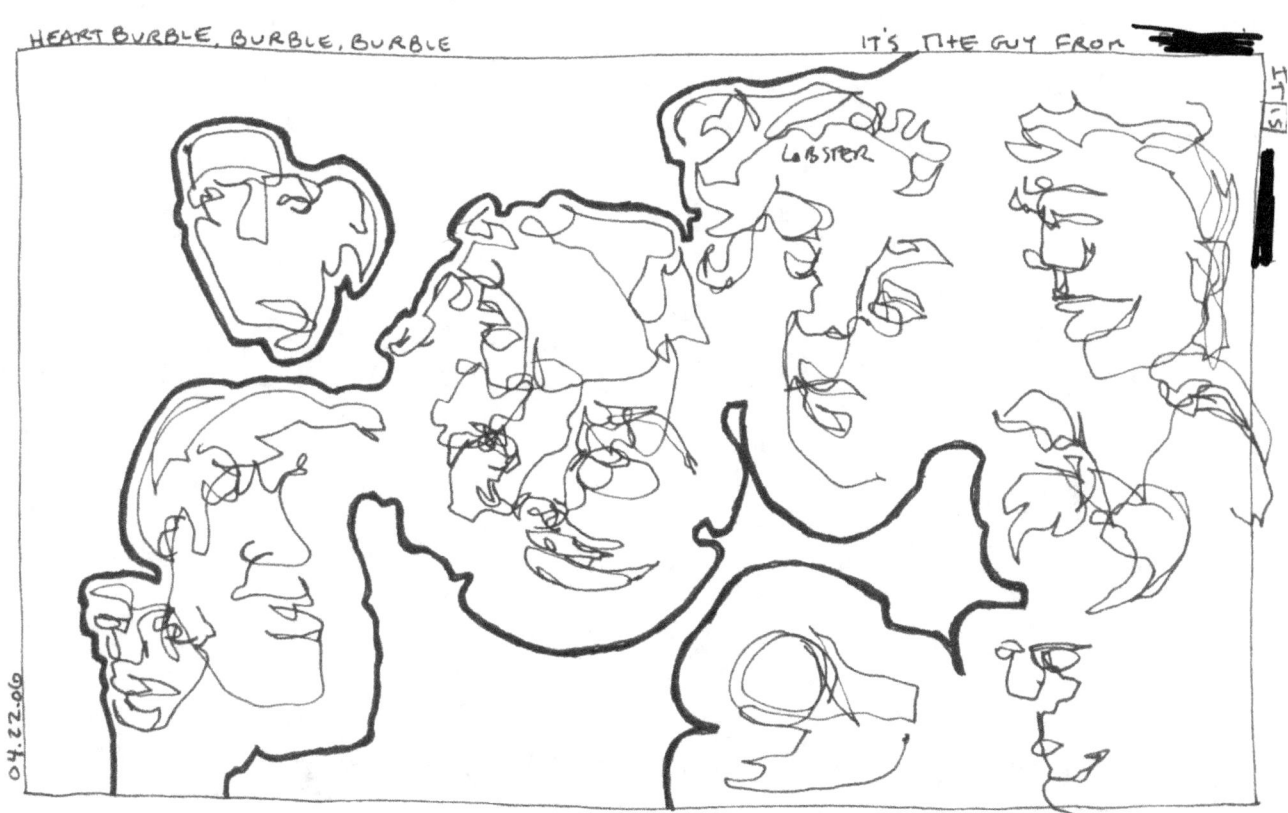

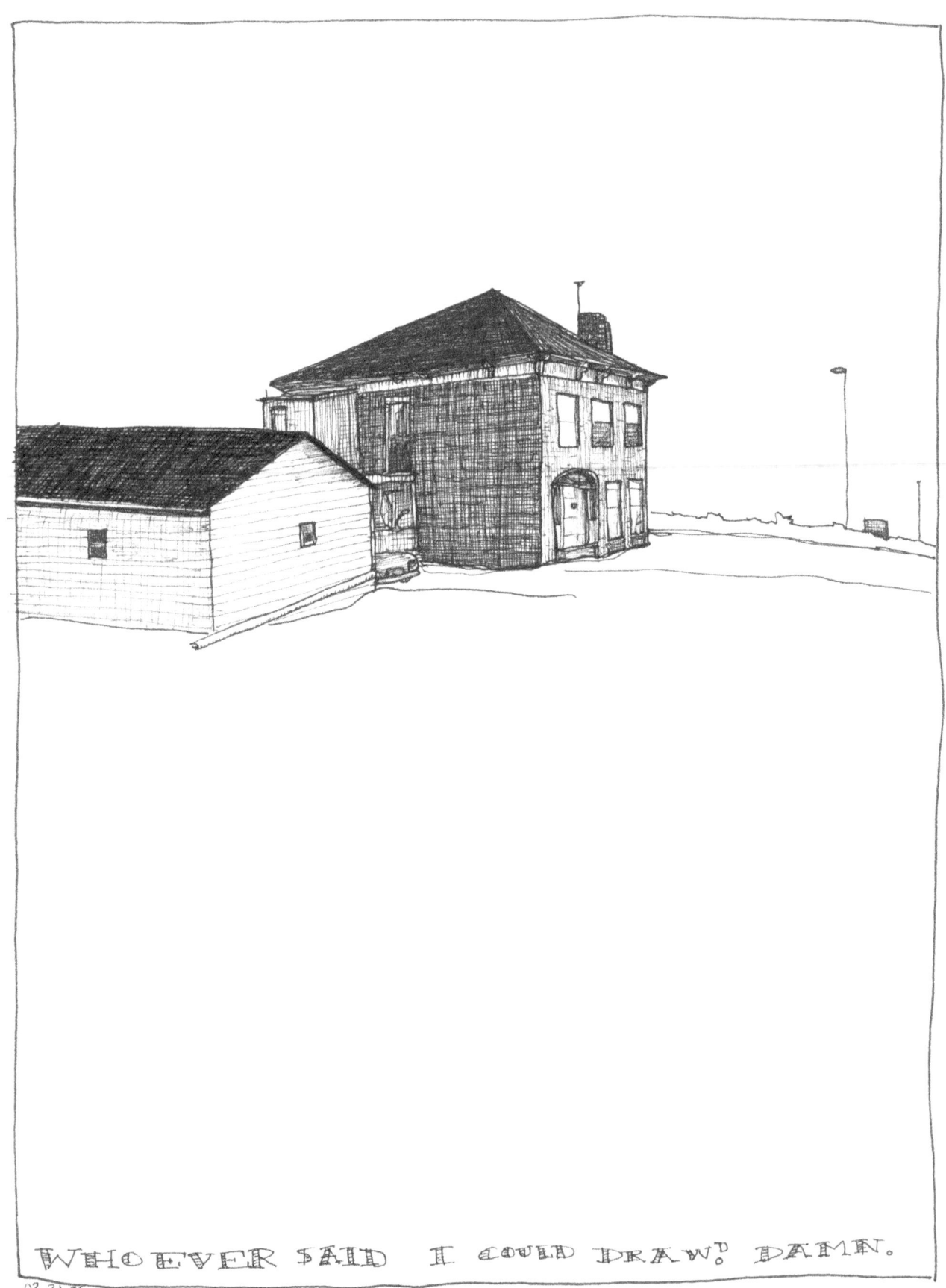

WHOEVER SAID I COULD DRAW? DAMN.

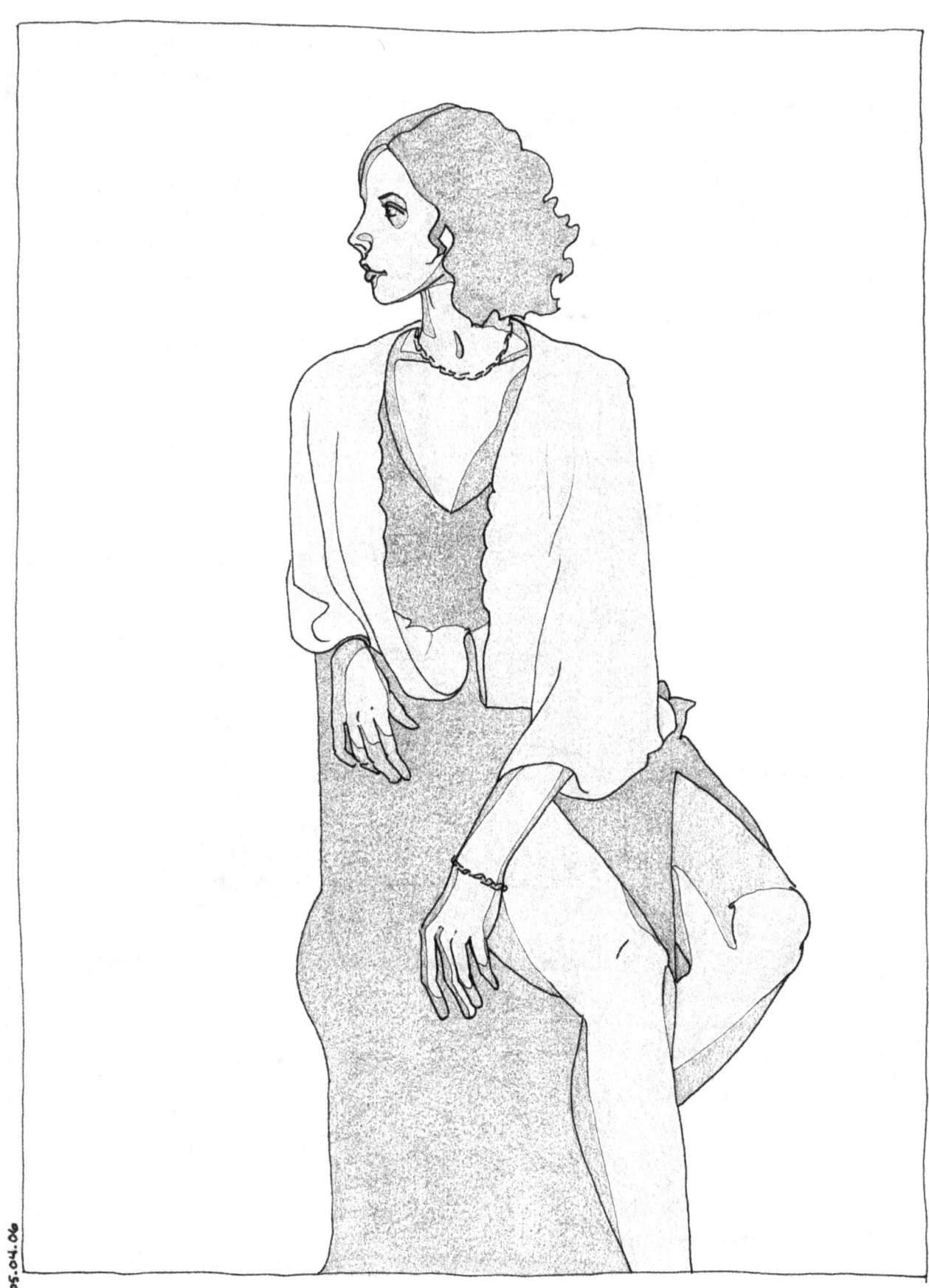

05.04.06

wide eyed, I saw myself in the mirror. It looked as though I had been crying but I couldn't remember anything. My face had three layers of shadows from the quality of light. I was half-mesmerized, half-frightened by my own look. I tried so hard to remember what had happened, who had hurt me, what I was doing there, who I was, where I was. Maybe it was a dream. Maybe I was asleep.

I know not when I came to seek you out. you were very young when I met you first. you had red-pink nose and green-blue eyes and black hair that had almost a purple tint to it. we were sitting by the river soaking up sound and sun when you looked at me and waited. I asked you what was the matter and you asked me if I had fed the cat last night. The cat was dying. It was older than me, however, so its oncoming death was no surprise. Still the cat continued breathing and eating and all of those other life necessities. You were so concerned with the cat's next step and you hounded me all the time to make sure everyday was just like the last. But it was something in the look you gave me and the pause that made your question so odd that day. It was as if you knew something I didn't and didn't want to say anything - you wanted to put it off. And so, answering yes, you turned away and went back to watching the river roll by. I sat and listened for something other than the sound of water...

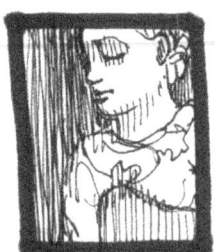

NAME FORGOTTEN...

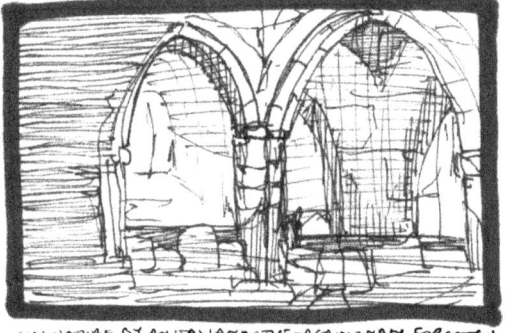

- MINIATURE BY AN ITALIAN ARTIST - AGAIN - NAME FORGOTTEN

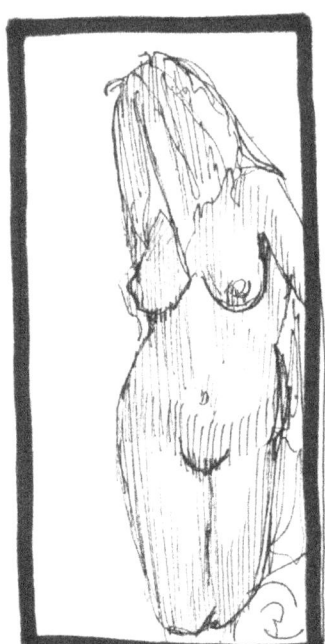

DRAWING BY AN ARTIST WHOSE NAME I FORGOT

I HAD HEARD A RUMOR THAT YOU WERE LEAVING TOWN. I FORGET WHERE YOU ENDED UP GOING, NOW THAT I THINK ABOUT IT. BUT, AT THE TIME, I WAS UNCONVINCED BECAUSE YOU HAD ALWAYS BEEN HERE. YOU ALWAYS WALKED THE SAME ROUTE TO THE BUS STOP AT THE SAME TIME EVERY DAY. YOU ORDERED THE SAME SANDWICH AT THE DELI ON A REGULAR SCHEDULE. YOU SMOKED THE SAME ROLLED CIGARETTES, CARRIED THE SAME PLASTIC BAG WITH GROCERIES, NODDED IN THE SAME MANNER WHEN EVER I WALKED PASSED. YOU COULDN'T LEAVE TOWN BECAUSE YOU WERE THE TOWN'S BREATH. THE RHYTHMIC INHALE AND EXHALE OF PEOPLE. I REMEMBER THE DAY THAT I NOTICED YOU WERE GONE VIVIDLY. I REMEMBER NOTICING THAT I WAS HOLDING MY BREATH.

THANK YOU

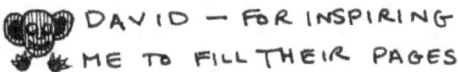 GIANNA — FOR GIVING ME THESE TWO SKETCH BOOKS

&

DAVID — FOR INSPIRING ME TO FILL THEIR PAGES

o ——————————— o